4997

FEB 28 '89

J
B
ADA

Stefoff, Rebecca 4997
John Adams: 2nd
president of the
United States

IMPERIAL PUBLIC LIBRARY
P.O. BOX 307
IMPERIAL, TEXAS 79743

John Adams

2nd President of the United States

John Adams
2nd President of the United States

Rebecca Stefoff

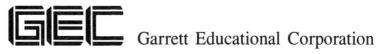 Garrett Educational Corporation

Cover: *Official portrait of John Adams by Edgar Parker.*
(Copyrighted by the White House Historical Association;
photograph by the National Geographic Society.)

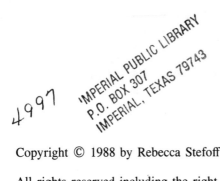

IMPERIAL PUBLIC LIBRARY
P.O. BOX 307
IMPERIAL, TEXAS 79743
4997

Copyright © 1988 by Rebecca Stefoff

All rights reserved including the right of reproduction in
whole or in part in any form without the prior written
permission of the publisher. Published by Garrett Educa-
tional Corporation, 130 East 13th Street, P.O. Box 1588,
Ada, Oklahoma 74820.

Manufactured in the United States of America

Edited and produced by Synthegraphics Corporation

Library of Congress Cataloging in Publication Data

Stefoff, Rebecca, 1951–
  John Adams, 2nd President of the United States.

  (Presidents of the United States)
  Bibliography: p.
  Includes index.
  Summary: Describes the childhood, education,
employment, and political career of America's second
president.
  1. Adams, John, 1735–1826—Juvenile literature.
2. Presidents—United States—Biography—Juvenile
literature. [1. Adams, John, 1735–1826. 2. Presidents]
I. Title. II. Series.
E322.S82 1988   973.4′4′0924 [B] [92]   87-32752
ISBN 0-944483-10-0

Contents

Chronology for John Adams

1735 Born on October 30

1751– Attended Harvard College
1755

1755– Taught school in Worcester,
1759 Massachusetts, while studying law

1759 Began to practice law in Braintree,
Massachusetts, after passing bar in
Boston

1764 Married Abigail Smith

1770 Defended British soldiers accused of
murder in Boston Massacre; began to
take growing part in patriotic movement

1774 Attended First Continental Congress in
Philadelphia

1776 Defended Declaration of Independence to
Congress

1776– Headed Congressional Board of War dur-
1777 ing Revolutionary War; recommended
George Washington as leader of Continental Army

1778 Went to France as part of a commission
to make treaties and trade agreements

1780– Negotiated treaty of recognition and loan
1782 with Dutch government

1782– Helped make peace between England and
1783 the United States

1785– Served as first American minister (am-
1788 bassador) to England

1789– **1797**	Served under George Washington as first Vice-President of the United States
1797– **1801**	Elected second President of the United States; made peace with France and established Department of the Navy
1801	Lost bid to win re-election; retired to Quincy
1818	Abigail died, his wife of 54 years
1826	Died on July 4, the same day that Thomas Jefferson died

This famous portrait by American artist John Singleton Copley shows Adams in his role as statesman during the 1780s. He is pointing to maps and a globe, the tools of the diplomat's trade. The classical figure in the background holds an olive branch, a symbol of peace. (Library of Congress.)

Chapter 1
The Puritan

On a moonless night in February of 1778, the middle of the Atlantic Ocean was torn by a violent storm. The seas rose higher and higher until the black waves were steep-sided monsters bigger than houses. A roaring wind lashed the tops of the huge waves into furies of flying foam.

In this confusion of wild rolling water, a small wooden ship struggled to stay afloat. It was dwarfed by the enormous waves that rose and fell on either side. Each time the ship plunged its bow into a wave, the decks streamed with tons of rushing water. The frantic seamen clung desperately to the ship's rigging to keep from being washed overboard and lost.

The ship was the *Boston*, an American vessel on its way to France. In those days, an ocean crossing was perilous indeed. Not only did high seas and unforeseen raging storms make travel dangerous (especially in the winter), but American vessels ran the risk of being captured by British ships. Since 1775, England and its American colonies had been at war. As a result, American ships were fair game, and sea chases and battles were common. Tonight, however, the *Boston* was alone on the storm-tossed sea. The weather worsened, and shortly before midnight Captain Welsh and his crew realized that they were in the middle of one of the most dreaded of all Atlantic storms, a nor'easter.

Below deck, in a cramped cabin, 43-year-old John Adams and his 10-year-old son braved the terrors of the storm together. It was the first ocean voyage for both—and tonight was not the first time they had felt fear during the crossing.

BRITISH PURSUIT

Earlier in the voyage, the *Boston* had been sighted by three British frigates. The British opened fire. When the *Boston* tried to escape, the British gave chase and demanded that Captain Welsh surrender. Although Adams put on a brave face for his son's benefit, he dreaded capture. He was on his way to France as a commissioner, a diplomat appointed by the revolutionary government in America to make treaties with the French. He knew that the British wanted to stop his mission, and that if he were captured, they would hang him for treason. Worst of all was his fear for his son: what would become of young John Quincy Adams if his father went to the scaffold in London?

Fortunately, the *Boston* outsailed two of its pursuers. The third British ship clung grimly to the chase until nightfall, when it and the *Boston* lost sight of one another. The danger of capture faded. But now the *Boston* and its crew and passengers faced a new danger—a terrible nor'easter.

As the hours passed, Adams and his son first tried to keep their minds off the storm by practicing their French together. Soon, though, the tossing of the ship in the savage seas made it impossible for them to read their grammar books. They had to put out their lantern for fear it would overturn and start a fire. In the pitch darkness, father and son clasped each other and braced their feet on the end of their bunk to keep from being dashed against the walls by the wild tossing of the ship.

The Storm Strikes a Blow

Suddenly, the roar of the storm was split by a tremendous cracking sound, followed by the shrill cries of the sailors.

Adams and his son gasped in alarm and clung more tightly to one another. The nor'easter had struck a deadly blow. The *Boston*'s mainmast had split from the gale-force pressure of the wind. It lay on the deck in a tangle of rigging, with its sails flapping uselessly. Captain Welsh had now lost much of the ship's steering power; all he could do was pray that the crippled ship would stay afloat until the storm waned.

Adams and young Johnny felt the change, as the ship's motion shifted from plunging forward through the waves to wallowing helplessly from side to side. Although he did not voice his fears, Adams knew that they were close to death. He tried to keep up Johnny's spirits by speaking calmly of events at home in Massachusetts, where Johnny's two brothers had taken over his chores on the family farm. He even joked that Johnny would speak better French than his father—when they arrived safe and sound in France.

This voyage, his first trip away from home, had been a great adventure for Johnny. He had pleaded to be allowed to accompany his father, and his mother had reluctantly agreed. Johnny had borne up well under all the hardships of the voyage. During the encounter with the British frigates, he had shown no fear—he even found the firing and the chase exciting. Now, however, he was genuinely frightened.

"Papa, what will happen to us?" he asked his father in a trembling voice as the ship pitched and rolled and the storm boomed around them.

"I do not know, Johnny, but I am certain that God will protect us."

"I wish we had never left home! Papa, *why* did you have to go to France?"

"You will understand when you are older, my son. It is my duty."

Finally, the storm died down and the seas grew calm. The ship's carpenter and the sailors repaired the mast, and the *Boston* made its way safely into the harbor at Bordeaux, France. But long after the terrors of the trip had become only memories of adventure, John Adams continued to act out of duty to his country. Duty, which for Adams meant doing what was right even at great cost to himself, was one of the forces that shaped his life. It was part of the Puritan heritage of the Adams family. To understand John Adams and his actions, it is helpful to know something about the Puritans and the virtues they believed in.

THE PURITAN HERITAGE

Puritanism arose in England during the 16th century, among people who believed that the Church of England needed to be "purified." The Puritans believed that some of the Church of England's practices and beliefs were becoming too much like those of the Catholic Church. Many Puritans broke away from the Church of England and formed new churches of their own. One of these was the Congregationalist Church of the Massachusetts Bay Colony in America.

The first Massachusetts colonists were Puritans and Congregationalists, and they hoped that their colony would remain Puritan forever. By the end of the 17th century, however, the Puritan grip on New England was weakening. The church no longer controlled all parts of public and private life, as it had in the early days of the colony. But during the 1730s, an important preacher and writer named Jonathan Edwards managed to stir up a new wave of strong Puritan feeling in Massachusetts.

Edwards urged people to return to the Puritan virtues of simplicity, honesty, spiritual strength to survive life's hardships, duty to God and one's fellow men, self-sacrifice, and orderliness. And for the next 10 or 20 years, religion and these Puritan values once again dominated life in New England, especially in Massachusetts. John Adams was born and raised during this time of Puritan devotion.

The Family Tree

John was the descendant of Henry Adams, a Puritan who had brought his wife to America in 1636 from the little town of Barton St. David in Somerset County, England. Upon arriving in the Massachusetts Bay Colony, Henry worked hard as a farmer on another man's acres. Two years later, he had saved enough money to buy his own farm of 40 acres near a hill called Mount Wollaston, in a community about 10 miles south of Boston that soon came to be called Braintree.

For many generations, Henry Adams' descendants remained in Braintree. They added more acreage to the original farm and built a brewery on the grounds. Many of them became church ministers and town officers. The Adamses were thought of as virtuous, hard-working, respectable people.

The third generation of Adamses to live in Braintree included Henry's grandson, the father of President John Adams. His name was John Adams, too. This John Adams was not only a farmer, he was also the town shoemaker and held many responsible posts in his church and town. He was a deacon (assistant minister) in the Braintree Congregational Church, where he served as a tithe collector (someone who collected the money owed by each family to the church, usually one-tenth of their total income). Deacon John Adams was also the local tax collector (he gave the tax money to the governor, who in turn sent it to England). Just before John Adams was born in 1735, Deacon Adams was elected to the town's board of selectmen, or managers.

As a result of all these activities, young John saw early in life how hard his father worked to carry out his service to the community. He grew up to share Deacon Adams' belief that service was an important responsibility. He also saw how

Both John Adams and his son, John Quincy Adams, were born on the original Adams homestead in Braintree, Massachusetts. John and Abigail set up housekeeping here — with help from servants — in 1764. (Library of Congress.)

much the townspeople looked up to and respected his father, and he hoped that someday he would be respected and admired as well.

A COLONIAL CHILDHOOD

John Adams was born to Deacon Adams and his wife, Susanna Boylston Adams, on October 30, 1735. He was their first child, and he was born in the old-fashioned New England farmhouse that Deacon John inherited from his grandfather, Henry Adams. Although the house had two stories, it had only one cramped room on each floor. A shed, called a "leanter," had been attached to one of the outside walls to form an extra room. Ceilings were low and windows were tiny, to make it easier for the log fires to heat the drafty rooms.

John Adams' younger years were much like those of any other boy born in the American colonies in the 1700s. It was an exciting time to be alive, full of adventure.

The colonists' settlement was limited to a thin strip of farms and towns along the coast, from Maine (which was then part of Massachusetts) south to the Carolinas. Just a few miles inland stretched the great wilderness: mile after mile of unmapped forest. During John's boyhood, no one knew the extent of that wilderness, or what it might contain. Although he never saw the true wilderness, young John shared the exciting fantasy of exploring the new continent as he listened to thrilling fireside tales about Indians and wild animals. As a boy, he was taken to visit some of the peaceful local Indians in their wigwams, and he was delighted when Indian chiefs and tribesmen visited his father to trade game and furs for shoes and other goods.

John's own boyhood travels were limited to occasional trips to his mother's family home in nearby Brookline, Massachusetts. He and his younger brothers—Peter, born in 1737, and Elihu, born in 1741—were awed by the large Boylston house. The Boylstons were a distinguished family with their own English coat of arms.

Favorite Youthful Pleasures

Mostly, however, John spent his time in Braintree, which, in the middle of the 1700s, was a country community made up of dozens of small farms. These were interrupted by out-croppings of granite rocks and clumps of thick forest, and by an abundance of streams, marshes, ponds, and lakes. John was rather chubby by the time he was 10. Although he had to huff and puff when he ran, he loved the outdoors. He took great pleasure in roaming through the woods and fields. He learned to hunt and fish when he was very young, and he later said that the thing he enjoyed most in life was hunting the ducks and other water birds that were plentiful in the area.

John also reveled in sports and games. Years later, he would describe his childhood like this:

> I spent my time as idle children do, in making and sailing boats and ships upon the ponds and brooks, in making and flying kites, in driving hoops, playing marbles, playing quoits, wrestling, swimming, skating, and above all shooting.

The usual time for these activities was after school or in the summer, but John wasn't above escaping from his classes to go for a ramble or a swim. Once, at age eight, he left his chores to go skating on a nearby pond with some older boys, who taught him how to smoke—a habit that stayed with him for the rest of his life.

The Deacon as a Role Model

In addition to its farms and homesteads, which were scat-tered over the nearby countryside, Braintree had at its center a cluster of buildings important to the community. There were at least two churches. One was the Congregational Church's meetinghouse, where John went with his family every Sunday. The meetinghouse was also used for town meetings, which were held about three or four times a year. As a selectman, Deacon Adams presided over some of these meetings. The other church was an Episcopal Church. It was closely related to the Church of England and was frowned on by people who came from a Puritan background, like the Adamses. Other buildings in the town included a number of taverns, which were called "tippling houses."

One of the most important buildings in Braintree was a house with the grand-sounding name of Mount Wollaston. It was the home of Colonel John Quincy, the town's leading social and political figure. The Quincy family was so important to the town that a part of Braintree was named Quincy when it became a separate town in 1792.

The Adamses and the Quincys were friendly with each other. Deacon Adams served as a lieutenant in the local militia, a force of men organized into an informal military troop in order to defend their homes and property from possible attack by the Indians or the French. One of the Quincys, named Josiah, was the colonel of the militia, which made him Deacon Adams' senior officer.

When John Adams was about 10, a rival officer managed to replace Quincy as colonel. This scheming newcomer offered John's father a promotion to the post of captain if he would agree to stay on in the militia. Deacon Adams scornfully refused, claiming that he owed his loyalty to Quincy, his "rightful" commander. Young John admired his father for giving up his post in the militia out of a sense of honor, and the Quincy family never forgot this loyal gesture. The two families became even closer friends. Years later, Deacon Adams' son John would bring the Adamses and the Quincys still closer together.

Chapter 2

The Student

John Adams was one of the most well-read men ever to serve as President of the United States. Reading and writing were his favorite pastimes throughout his adult life. As a boy, however, he hated school and was a poor student.

Deacon Adams believed in the value of education. His mother, called Grandmother Bass by young John Adams, loved books. Years later, John would remember that she read a great deal more than most other women of her day, and that her family had always respected her wisdom. Deacon Adams' older brother, Joseph, had graduated from Harvard College in nearby Cambridge, Massachusetts. Joseph Adams had then taught school in Braintree before becoming a minister in New Hampshire. Deacon Adams admired his older brother's learning and achievements. He was determined that his oldest son would follow the same path.

A SHORT-LIVED CAREER

Young John had other ideas, however. In spite of his admiration for Grandmother Bass, he had no great love of books. Deacon Adams and Susanna first taught John the alphabet. Then, as a small child, he attended a private school in the home of a neighbor, Mrs. Belcher, whose husband was also a deacon in the Congregational Church. There John learned to read so well that at age seven he read a list of advice for children written out by Grandmother Bass.

After several years of Mrs. Belcher's teaching, John was sent to the local public school. The teacher, whose name was Joseph Cleverly, taught his pupils Latin. At that time, every educated person learned how to read and write Latin, and subjects such as history were often taught in the Latin language. John didn't like Cleverly, who sometimes scolded him for playing truant in order to shoot and fish. When his father scolded John for his poor school performance, John retorted that Cleverly was lazy and a bad teacher.

Finally when John was about 10 years old, his father grew impatient that John was not making the most of his opportunity to get an education. Knowledge of Latin, Deacon Adams pointed out, was a necessary requirement for anyone who wanted to study at Harvard College. John knew of his father's plans for him to go to Harvard and become a minister, and he did not share them. "I don't need an education," John hotly declared. "I'm not going to go to Harvard."

Rather than lose his temper, Deacon Adams simply asked, "What will you do?"

"I'll be a farmer."

"A farmer?" his father replied. "Very well, I'll show you what it is to be a farmer."

Early the next morning, Deacon Adams woke his son and took him to a damp, marshy area known as Penny Ferry to cut thatch (straw and reeds used to make roofs for barns and sheds). It proved to be a long day of difficult, muddy work, and the plump John was panting with exhaustion when it finally became too dark to keep working. As Deacon Adams and his son tramped home through the fields, the father asked, "Well, son, are you satisfied with being a farmer?"

"I like it very well, sir," said the boy.

"Aye, but I don't like it so well," was all Deacon Adams answered. "Tomorrow you go back to school."

John gave up his defiant stand, but asked to go to a different school. At first his father would not agree, but eventually, when John was about 14, he was permitted to leave Cleverly's class and study at a private school.

His new school was run by a Mr. Marsh, a minister's son who was known for preparing his students to pass the entrance examinations at Harvard College. Many of his pupils had attended the college, and Deacon Adams was still determined that John would also go there.

From Stubborn to Scholarly

John studied with Marsh for about a year and a half. During this time, he immersed himself in history, especially the history of England. He also dedicated himself to his Latin studies and even studied arithmetic on his own. Once he had decided to follow his father's wishes and complete his education, John felt that he might as well go all the way and turn himself into a serious scholar. The habits of reading and essay-writing that he developed under Marsh stayed with him for the rest of his life.

When he was 16, John was ready to be interviewed at Harvard College. (In those days, young men who wanted to attend Harvard were interviewed in person by the college's president and tutors.) The interview got off to a bad start. Although Marsh was supposed to be present to introduce John and to tell what a good pupil he had been, he failed to appear. This was to be the first of several times John Adams would be let down or embarrassed by people he trusted. He made the best of it, though, and introduced himself with great self-confidence. Then he was asked to take the entrance examination.

The examination was a passage in Latin that John was supposed to translate into English. He sat down full of confidence, but as soon as he saw the passage, his heart sank.

Adams attended Harvard College in Cambridge, Massachusetts, about 25 years after this engraving by William Burgis was published. Although Harvard is much larger today, many of the buildings of Adams' time still stand. (Library of Congress.)

It was one of the most difficult Latin passages he had ever seen, full of strange words whose meanings were a complete mystery to him. Just when he was sure he'd never be able to pass the test, he was told that he could use a dictionary! He then passed the test satisfactorily and returned to Braintree with great news: he was going to go to Harvard.

COLLEGE YEARS

Harvard College had been founded by the Puritans as an outpost of learning in the American colonies. It was a training ground for most of the teachers and ministers of New England. But although the town of Cambridge was the center of higher education and intellectual life in the colonies, it was just as rural as Braintree. Many of the professors lived on farms; many even kept cows.

When John arrived at Harvard, there were about 90 students at the college. The school's president was Edward Holyoke, whom the students called "Old Guts." Holyoke was a distinguished Latin scholar and theologian (a scholar of religion). He expected his students to live up to strict codes of gentlemanly and Puritan behavior, and he fined them if they broke any of the rules. Anyone caught swearing, for example, had to pay a five-shilling fine. But in spite of Old Guts and his fines, some of the wealthier and more high-spirited students drank, played cards, and even sneaked over to Boston without permission from time to time. Like colleges today, Harvard in the 1750s could appeal to both the sober, industrious student and the fun-loving young man.

John Adams entered Harvard in the fall of 1751. From the start, he was one of the sober, hard-working students, although he did not win distinction as a brilliant scholar. At the end of his first year, he was ranked 14th in a class of 28, which displeased his mother, who felt he should be closer to the top of the list.

A Student's Life
Was Not an Easy One

Life at Harvard during John Adams' years there followed a rigid pattern. Adams lived in Massachusetts Hall for all four years. All of his classes were in nearby Harvard Hall. Like students today, Adams spent a lot of time running from his room to his classes to the library.

Each day began at 6:00 A.M. with prayers. Breakfast was bread and milk, but some of the wealthy students added eggs and bacon to the college meal. Classes were held from 8:00 A.M. until noon, when a meal of meat and vegetables was served. After lunch, students had two hours of outdoor activities, rain or shine. Evening prayers were held at 5:00 P.M., and woe to the poor student who missed them! Supper (smaller than the noon meal) was then served, after which the students retired to their rooms for study by candlelight.

All of the bathrooms were outdoors and unheated. Inside, heat came from log fires, and the students had to provide their own wood. John's brother Peter made frequent trips from Braintree to Cambridge with wood, but there never seemed to be enough to keep John's drafty room warm.

Freshmen and sophomores studied logic, Latin, Greek, and rhetoric (the use of language and grammar). Juniors and seniors continued these studies, but added mathematics, history, literature, physics, and

> "natural history" (a mixture of biology, anatomy, and meteorology). To top it off, all students received lessons in religion from President Holyoke every Saturday morning.

Once, during his sophomore year, John received a visit from his mother and one of her sisters. They were dismayed to see how bare and plain his room was, lacking in any little luxuries or conveniences. John explained that he lived as cheaply as possible because he did not want to burden his father with extra expenses.

The young student enjoyed his years at Harvard. "I soon perceived a growing curiosity, a love of books and a fondness for study," he wrote later, adding that his enjoyment of his studies was so great that he no longer cared for sports, or even for meeting girls at parties and other social events.

Extracurricular Activities

John spent most of his winter and summer vacations at home in Braintree, reading and preparing for his next classes. In the summer of 1753, however, he traveled with a cousin to Uncle Joseph Adams' house in Newington, New Hampshire. There he told his uncle about his classes at Harvard and listened to tales of Joseph Adams' student days.

At the start of his junior year, John was invited to join a "play-reading club." It was something like today's debating societies. Club members not only read plays and poems aloud, they also made speeches about school subjects and current events. John quickly developed a flair for public speaking. He liked dramatic subjects, ones that allowed him to use vigorous gestures and expressions. In later years, he recalled that he was often asked to read, "especially tragedies," as he said. He took great pride in the fact that the other club members admired his speaking skills. Those skills would prove useful in his career and would one day earn him the nickname "the Atlas of Independence."

In his senior year, as graduation neared, John began a diary. The practice of keeping a diary or daily journal was very common among the Puritans of New England. Puritans were urged to keep a daily record of their faults and short-comings, and to set goals to improve themselves. This detailed self-examination sometimes turned into an examination of other people—sometimes, in fact, it contained a great deal of what modern writers would call gossip. Much of what we know about the early years of the American colonies comes from piecing together the details of daily life found in hundreds of Puritan diaries.

John Adams actually started his diary because of an earthquake. He had developed an interest in scientific subjects, including the study of the weather. When a mild earthquake shook Cambridge in 1755, he could not resist making a few notes about it. Soon he had formed the habit of recording each day's weather in a few words. Then he began to add a few more words, listing the books he was reading, and sometimes copying down a few lines that he found particularly interesting in one of them.

This type of journal, containing observations on reading or other subjects without any personal matter, is sometimes called a commonplace book. John would soon begin to use his journal for the Puritan purpose of examining himself for spiritual failings. He kept up his diary, with a few lapses, for many years. It is now an important source of information about his life and personality.

THE MINISTRY'S LOSS

One subject that John wrestled with in his diary was his decision not to enter the ministry. From the time he was born, his father had planned for John to become a minister. He had been sent to Harvard to prepare him for that very career. When he graduated in the spring of 1755 with a bachelor of arts degree, his family and friends expected him to take up theological studies. Yet John himself had made up his mind early on that he did not want to be a minister.

In spite of his lifelong religious training, starting with daily prayers led by his father, John Adams does not seem to have had very strong religious feelings. He felt that religion was important because it led to order and responsible behavior, but he knew that he lacked the spark of faith and enthusiasm that a good preacher needs. During his Harvard years, he had begun to consider other careers. Indeed, without telling his parents, he had begun to prepare for a career outside the church by studying more literature, mathematics, science, and history than religion.

Although he had not lost his love for the country life, John no longer wanted to be a simple farmer. His newfound love of learning inspired him to search for a career that would make use of his education—and allow him to continue it. His successes as a public speaker had fired his ambition, and he admitted in his diary that he wanted to do something important, to make a mark in the world.

Thus, upon graduating John was faced with two difficult tasks. First, he had to tell his parents that he did not intend to become a minister. Second, he had to decide upon a career and a course of action for himself. He then remembered that his uncle, Joseph Adams, had been a schoolteacher for a while before he became a minister. John Adams decided he would do the same. He would become a schoolteacher. Before long, he was sure, he would be setting his feet on a more ambitious road.

Chapter 3

The Lawyer

A t his Harvard graduation ceremony, Adams took part in a debate, as was the custom for all graduating students. He chose as his topic "Liberty cannot exist without law." His powerful argument that laws were needed to keep liberty from being mere chaos shows that he may already have begun to consider a career in law.

At any rate, his performance at the graduation impressed the Congregationalist minister of Worcester, Massachusetts. When he heard that John was looking for a schoolteaching job, the minister offered him a teaching position at the grammar school in Worcester. In the summer of 1755, John arrived in Worcester to take up his new duties.

EARLY CAREER AS A SCHOOLMASTER

Located 40 miles from Braintree, Worcester was then a town of about 1,500 people. Because it was rare at that time for young, unmarried people to have homes of their own or to live alone, Adams followed the usual practice of boarding with the town's families. Often, he was invited out for afternoon tea with one family before having the evening meal in the house where he was staying. Before long, he knew everyone in town and had fallen into a new daily routine similar to the one he had followed at Harvard.

John continued to read every book he could, especially books about politics, and he began copying and translating long passages from his readings. He also continued the habit of regular diary-keeping. His diary entries from this time show a curious and sometimes comical mixture of his old interest in the weather and his growing desire to analyze his own character. A typical entry from early 1756 reads like this: "Serene weather, but somewhat cool. I am constantly forming, but never executing, good resolutions."

One subject that began to appear in his diary at about this time was his health. Although he was to live to the ripe old age of 90, Adams never felt that he was truly healthy. Like many people in the 18th century, he believed that a person's illness or health had a lot to do with the climate and atmosphere, or "the air." He began to miss the salty sea air and brisk breezes of Braintree, and he complained that Worcester's "bad air" made him feel tired and weak. But the 18th century, like the 20th, had its share of fad diets and miracle cures. Sometime during his stay in Worcester, Adams learned of one popular diet that was supposed to restore health and energy. It was called Dr. Cheyney's Diet, and it consisted of nothing but bread and milk. For the rest of his life, Adams would turn to Dr. Cheyney's Diet whenever he felt ill — although he was never able to stay on the diet for very long.

Thus it was that 10 years after his days at Joseph Cleverly's school, John Adams was himself now a schoolmaster. And, as it happened, he was guilty of the same faults as Cleverly, whom he had accused of being idle and not paying enough attention to him. Now, as some of his pupils would later remember, John spent most of the school day writing papers of his own or daydreaming. Most of the time, he managed the school by making the older and smarter students teach the younger and duller ones. It didn't take John long to realize that he was no more interested in teaching than in preaching.

BECOMING A LAWYER

In 1756, Adams ended the uncertainty about his career. He announced that he was going to become a lawyer. Because of his interest in speech-making and in law and government, John's decision was not a great surprise to his family. Nevertheless, his mother and father were disappointed. Deacon Adams had always cherished the hope that his son would enter the ministry. Susanna Boylston Adams, on the other hand, held the common belief of the time that the law was not quite a respectable profession for a gentleman. And both parents knew that, in the 18th century, lawyers often had a hard time making enough money to live on.

Having made the difficult decision to become a lawyer, John was now determined and excited. His first step was to move into the home of James Putnam, a Worcester man whom many considered to be the best lawyer in the colonies. Adams was first Putnam's pupil, then his assistant. The two men spent hours discussing weighty law topics and arguing about cases and evidence. Their dinner-table conversation revolved around questions of politics and religion.

To pay his bills, Adams continued to hold his job as schoolmaster by day. By night, he spent long hours studying. In the spring of 1756, a year after receiving his bachelor's degree, Adams earned his master of arts degree from Harvard by the simple means of making a speech at the graduation exercises.

Unlike his father, Adams never joined the militia or took part in any kind of warfare. During his Worcester years, however, he witnessed a great deal of military activity. The French and Indian War (1754–1763) was being fought in Canada and on the frontier, and British troops often passed through Worcester. Even colonists who had begun to resent England's rule put aside their hostile feelings and rooted for the British to win the war. British victories usually called for celebrations throughout the colonies. Local militias grew in size and importance, and for a while Lawyer Putnam was also the commander of a local militia.

During the two and a half years he studied with Putnam, Adams came to admire the older man's learning and skill. Eventually, however, he became convinced that Putnam was secretly hostile to him, perhaps because he feared a future rival. At any rate, Adams soon began to make fun of Putnam in his diary. He called him "Old Put," although Putnam was only eight or ten years older. And in early 1759, when the time came for Adams to end his apprenticeship and become a lawyer, he found his suspicions of Putnam were correct.

In order to practice law, Adams had to be certified by the Boston bar. Because he applied for permission to practice in the Court of Common Pleas in Suffolk County, which included Braintree and Boston, he had to go to Boston to be admitted to the bar. When he got there, he found that Putnam, like Marsh years before, had let him down. Putnam had neglected to give his pupil any letters of recommendation. This embarrassed Adams and caused a temporary difficulty, but the examiners were eventually convinced of Adams' credentials. He was made a member of the bar and was now ready to start on his new profession.

RETURN TO BRAINTREE

Even though they were disappointed with his choice of profession, John's parents invited him to return home to begin practicing law. They knew that it would be hard for him to support himself while starting out. For his part, John was happy to go home. He missed the "good air" of Braintree, which was to remain his favorite place for the rest of his life. Perhaps, too, he realized that he might never have any clients in Worcester, where everyone regarded his former teacher as the best lawyer around.

There may have been another reason for John's eagerness to return to Braintree. Samuel Quincy, one of John's best friends from Harvard and the son of old Colonel Josiah Quincy (whom Deacon Adams had served under in the militia) also lived in Braintree. And Samuel had a beautiful sister, Hannah Quincy, who was notorious as a flirt and a heartbreaker, even in those proper Puritan times. Two of Adams' closest Braintree friends, Parson Anthony Wibird and Richard Cranch, had already fallen under her spell. Then, during his frequent visits to Braintree from Worcester, Adams also fell in love with her.

Upon arriving in Braintree in 1759, Adams devoted himself to two things: trying to win Hannah's attention away from her many other admirers, and starting his new business. He had no success with Hannah, however, and little success with business.

Because of his friendship with Sam Quincy and the friendly relationship between their two families, Adams was often in and out of the Quincy house. He had numerous chances to see Hannah, and he wrote in his diary that he was ruined for business or study because he spent all his time thinking about the girl.

In later years, Adams let it be known that he had almost proposed to Hannah – but that he had decided against it because common sense told him that the expense and responsibilities of marriage would put too great a strain on his shaky new career. He wanted it to appear that *he* had decided against marriage for practical reasons. He even recorded in his diary that he had given up Hannah to devote himself to his work, writing, "The thing is ended. A tender scene! A great sacrifice to reason!"

Some of this self-sacrifice was probably true. There is

no doubt that Adams believed marriage just then would be disastrous for his career, which was barely off the ground. But he surely knew that Hannah didn't return his feelings. At least part of the reason he didn't propose to her must have been because he knew she would have turned him down. He preferred to think of himself as making a noble sacrifice rather than as a rejected suitor. When Hannah married someone else the following year, Adams finally stopped thinking about her.

The Young Lawyer's First Case

Adams had other problems and disappointments to fill his thoughts. Because there were many other lawyers in the Braintree and Boston area (his friend, Sam Quincy, was one), it was difficult for a young man new to the law to get cases and clients. To make matters worse, his first case was a failure.

It involved two local farmers, Luke Lambert and Joseph Field, neighbors who had carried on a series of feuds for years. When two of Lambert's horses broke into Field's pasture, Field kept the horses, saying that he would not release them until Lambert paid for the damage they caused. Lambert then carried out a "rescue raid" and retrieved his horses. Now, about two months after his return to Braintree, Adams was hired by Field to sue Lambert. Lambert's lawyer was Sam Quincy, and the presiding justice of the peace was Josiah Quincy, Sam and Hannah's father.

At the time Field hired him, Adams was deeply involved in studying some extremely difficult books on Roman and Dutch law. He was doing this in spite of some friendly advice from one of the town's leading older lawyers, who suggested that John would find it more profitable if he concentrated on local statutes for a while. Adams really did not have the slightest idea how to draw up Field's writ (legal papers). He didn't want to take the case, but he did so for two reasons: first, his mother was upset that he might turn down the first piece of business to come his way in two months, and second, he was afraid people would think he didn't know how to draw up the writ.

As it turned out, his fears came true. The writ did indeed contain some technical errors; for example, Adams had forgotten to include in it the name of the county. Because of these errors, the writ was dismissed from court, Field didn't get a penny from Lambert, and Adams was embarrassed by losing his first case—and a simple one, at that. Later, he admitted in his diary that he had been wrong to spend all his time on subjects that interested him and none on matters that would be important to his clients. He felt that he had failed in his duty to Field and to himself. He was particularly hard on himself for having boasted to his friends about reading a difficult book on obscure Dutch law just weeks before his failure in court.

Regaining Stature as a Lawyer

His father's death in 1761 saddened Adams. It also meant that he, as the oldest son, had to help with the family responsibilities once more. He rediscovered the joys of farming, although he did not take his father's place on the farm. Instead, his brother Peter inherited most of the farm and the old family house (Adams bought it from him years later). Elihu received a smaller farm nearby. John, who had been given an education and had a profession, received a smaller house next to the family homestead.

While these family matters were being sorted out, Adams was slowly building a business. In spite of his poor showing in the Field-Lambert case, he began to receive commissions for preparing writs for many minor cases. He realized it was not likely that he would soon make a public name in a great, dramatic case. Instead, he knew that he would have to take a lot of little cases for small fees. He dutifully studied the details of local law and court procedure; as a result, he was successful in many of his cases.

Although he realized that his work for the time being would be more concerned with writs and deeds than with the theories of law he had read so much about, Adams couldn't resist the impulse to bring some of his learning and reading into humble courtroom affairs. Once a judge leaned across the table and ordered him to "keep to the evidence . . . don't ramble all over the world." Adams tried to obey, but fate occasionally gave him opportunities for drama.

In one case, for example, he discovered in court that his client had forgotten to bring a document that might be required. Remembering how he had lost the Field case because of small technical errors, Adams was determined that he wouldn't lose this one for a similar reason. He instructed his client to ride home and get the document. When the worried client protested that it would take him a long time to go home and return, Adams told him not to worry and sent him on his way. When the time came for Adams to make a speech summing up his client's case, he rose and talked for five hours, without reference books or preparation, until his client came running into the courtroom waving the paper. Finally, all the years Adams had spent absorbing legal histories and obscure cases found an outlet in this amazing five-hour speech.

Adams began to be a person of some stature in the community. People admired his learning and respected his hard work on behalf of his clients. His recommendation helped get his brother Peter appointed deputy sheriff in 1761. Adams himself was elected a selectman at a town meeting, as his father had been before him. He was also made town surveyor, a post that made him responsible for laying out roads and dividing land that belonged to the township. Adams took these municipal responsibilities quite seriously. Even in later years, when he was often away from home for years at a time, he prided himself on being a good citizen of Braintree.

AMBITION AND AUTHORSHIP

As his law practice began to take root in the early 1760s, Adams started working toward another goal: he wanted to achieve recognition as a writer. By this time, newspapers had become well established in the American colonies, and most cities and towns had their own papers. In those days, newspapers contained – in addition to the news – many essays and letters written by the educated and prominent men of the community. Because Adams wanted to be numbered among these men, he was consumed by a burning desire to write for the papers.

Of course, Adams had been writing for himself for years, in his lecture notes, diary, summaries of books he had read, essays, and, most recently, legal statements. Now he felt he was ready to parade his learning and serious-mindedness before an audience of readers. "A pen," he wrote in his diary, "is certainly an excellent instrument to fix a man's attention and inflame his ambitions."

He admitted to himself that he was ambitious, and his diary for the years 1761 and 1762 tells us that he spent much time and effort wrestling with his thoughts about fame and ambition. He needed to decide whether his fiery desire for fame and greatness was a noble ambition (if it was in the service of his fellow men) or a selfish, vain one (if it was only to seek glory for its own sake). He finally decided that there was nothing to be ashamed of in wanting recognition for worthy deeds – and sharing his educated and intelligent thoughts for the benefit of the community must certainly be considered a worthy deed! For the rest of his life, Adams constantly examined his heart, in the Puritan tradition of self-criticism, to see whether his actions and feelings came from honest ambition or vanity. It was a question he was never able to answer to his complete satisfaction.

At first, however, his ambitions to be an author were frustrated. He scribbled frantically by day and night, turning out dozens of essays and letters. He intended to publish them anonymously (not giving his name as the author), which was the fashion of the time. Newspaper articles were unsigned, or their authors used made-up names, sometimes humorous or Latin ones. Eventually, if the public continued to respond favorably to his articles, the author would let it be "leaked" among his acquaintances that *he* was, in fact, "A Concerned Citizen" or "Mr. Good-News," or whatever his chosen pen name had been.

Most of Adams' writing attempts during this period were stern moral attacks on taverns, or "tippling houses." He presented them as hotbeds of vice, debt, and civic disruption. He would, however, write on anything that he thought might make its way into the columns of a newspaper. Once he even wrote a letter, addressed "Dear Nieces," that gave rules for etiquette and proper social behavior for young ladies!

Despite his energy and his broad range of subjects, Adams was at first unsuccessful in getting published. One entry in his diary for this period shows that Adams agreed with Benjamin Prat, a Boston lawyer and philosopher, who said that old people never think young people have any judgment. Perhaps, Adams feared, the newspaper editors thought he was too young and inexperienced to take seriously.

Finally, however, in March of 1763 the Boston *Evening Post* printed several humorous articles by Adams about the problems of New England farmers. People were interested in such subjects at the time because a recent book, called *Essays on Field Husbandry Especially in New England,* had been very popular. Adams' articles were written in a rustic (backwoods or country) dialect and signed "Humphrey Ploughjogger." They combined humor with a real understanding of farming life. Readers must have liked them, because the series was continued through the summer. During that same summer, the Boston *Gazette* published two serious essays by Adams on moral subjects, "Private Revenge" and "Self-Delusion."

While he was beginning to enjoy the satisfaction of writing for the newspapers, Adams was also entering a new stage in his emotional life. He had fallen in love and was thinking about marriage.

AN 18TH-CENTURY COURTSHIP

Once again, Adams was in love with a Quincy girl. This time she was Hannah Quincy's cousin, Abigail Quincy Smith. The Smith girl lived in nearby Weymouth, Massachusetts, where her father, the Reverend William Smith, was the minister of the Congregational Church. Her mother, Elizabeth Quincy, was the daughter of Colonel John Quincy of Braintree.

Abigail, or Nabby, as her family and friends called her, was a slender, brown-eyed girl who was quieter and more serious than many of her friends. Because her mother believed that Nabby was unhealthy, or "delicate," she never attended school. Grandmother Quincy, who lived in the big Mount Wollaston house in Braintree, took the place of school. Abigail later recalled that her grandmother had used "a happy method of mixing instruction and amusement together" to teach her to read and write. During her childhood, Nabby spent a lot of time at her grandparents' home in Braintree. She must have known John Adams, who was nine years older than she, but they took no notice of each other until about 1761, when Nabby was 17 and Adams was 26.

Then, more than a year after he had "given Hannah up," Adams began to call on Hannah's cousin. He may have visited the Smith family first with his friend Richard Cranch, who was courting Nabby's older sister Mary. Before long, however, Adams began to enjoy talking to Nabby, who surprised him with her soft-spoken but firm opinions on politics and other serious matters. She had a strong belief in the rights of women, a subject that was considered somewhat outlandish at the time, and Adams could see that she was thoughtful and straightforward, perhaps a welcome change from Hannah's playful flirting.

In the 18th century, it was rare for young men and women to see each other often unless they intended to marry. "Dating" was unheard of; it was considered improper for boys and girls to be together without a chaperone. Relationships between the sexes were a serious matter and were supposed to lead to just one thing: marriage. This is how someone like Hannah Quincy could earn a reputation for flirting and fickleness by behavior that would seem quite harmless today.

In keeping with this solemn approach to affairs of the heart, Adams decided soon after he began calling on Nabby in 1761 that they would marry. She had the qualities he desired in a wife, he felt, and soon his business would enable him to support two people. In addition, she took an interest in matters important to him, such as law and politics. In short, he loved her. Now all that remained was to see whether she would have him.

There was one important obstacle in his way, however. Nabby's mother, Elizabeth Quincy Smith, disapproved of John Adams as a suitor. She had heard stories of his attachment to Hannah Quincy, and she did not want it said that he had turned to Abigail after Hannah jilted him. She also felt that a young, struggling lawyer was not a very promising match for a girl from the prosperous Quincy clan. But Nabby's father, who liked and respected Adams, was on the young couple's side. He welcomed Adams' increasingly frequent visits to the Smith home, and even found a few opportunities to take his wife out of the parlor so that John and Abigail could talk alone together.

After a few months of these visits, John declared his love and, to his delight, Nabby agreed to marry him. Both of them knew, however, that they would have to wait until John had established himself in his law practice and saved some money. They were prepared to wait several years, because long engagements were normal at that time.

Love Letters Shorten the Wait

Because there was no telephone or telegraph, and because even short trips were difficult in those days of horseback travel and muddy roads, many courting couples did not see each other as often as they wished. Adams and his Abigail were no different. Although Adams managed to visit Weymouth at least once a month, the two spent the several years of their engagement getting to know one another better by the usual 18th-century method of letter-writing. In those days, writing letters was a skill, a pleasure, or a responsibility in everyone's life. Many people regularly wrote two or three letters a day, every day of their lives.

Of course, Adams enthusiastically turned his love of writing to the task of writing love letters, and Nabby turned out to be a wonderful letter-writer; in later years, in fact, her letters were highly prized by the friends who received them, and many of her letters to John and others have been published. So the two young lovers set to work with pen and paper, and a long series of affectionate, often passionate letters resulted. It was common at that time for people who wrote frequently to each other to adopt nicknames, usually from classical (Greek or Roman) literature or history. The names that Adams and Nabby chose say something about their characters. Nabby called herself "Diana," after the Roman goddess of light, learning, and chastity. Adams called himself "Lysander," taking the name of a famous Greek general who was also a diplomat and a public leader. The fact that he used a name associated with fame and government rather than one connected with romance shows how important his ambitions had become.

The Smallpox Scare

Adams and Abigail had one serious scare during their engagement: an epidemic of smallpox broke out in Boston, killing dozens of people. Smallpox was a serious illness in the 18th century, and people were terrified of catching it. Many in Braintree and the other towns around Boston feared that it would spread. Because he often rode into Boston on court business, John was in danger of catching the disease and spreading it to Braintree or Weymouth. Rather than giving up his business in Boston, which by now was an important part of his income, Adams decided to take the risky step of undergoing the new inoculation treatment, which involved deliberately infecting a person with a mild version of smallpox. A special "pox hospital" (also called the "pest house") had been opened in Boston to carry out the inoculation, which was believed to prevent smallpox—if the patient lived through it.

For about a month after the inoculation, the person who had been deliberately infected was treated with diet, medicines, and even surgery to remove the resulting pox sores. It was a painful, unpleasant experience with uncertain results, but Adams believed it to be his duty. He took himself off to Boston and was shut up in the pox hospital. He survived with no ill effects, and he wrote frequently to Nabby from his sickbed. Nabby's mother made her hold his letters in the smoke from the fireplace before opening them, fearing her daughter could catch smallpox from the paper.

A Wedding at Last

The engagement promise of John Adams and Abigail Smith was finally kept on October 25, 1764. They were married in

The kitchen in John and Abigail's first house was restored by the Quincy Historical Society in the late 19th century. Heavy iron pots over a log fire made up the typical kitchen of the Colonial era. (Library of Congress.)

Weymouth by Abigail's father, who created a mild sensation at the wedding by his choice of text from the Bible.

The Reverend Smith had a habit of collecting sayings and biblical quotes and using them in ways he thought were funny—although his listeners did not always agree. He had preached a humorous sermon at the wedding of his daughter Mary to Richard Cranch two years before, to the astonishment of some members of the congregation. Now, at Abigail's wedding, he chose this Bible verse: "And John came neither eating bread nor drinking wine, and ye say, *He hath a devil*" *(Luke 7:33–34)*. The guests gasped and craned their necks to stare at the bridegroom, but the joke didn't interfere with John's happiness. He was about to start the adventure of married life. What he couldn't know was that he and Abigail would be married for 54 years of challenges, triumphs, and tragedies. Future friends and acquaintances would describe the marriage of John and Abigail as an ideally happy partnership.

Chapter 4

The Patriot

After the wedding, John and Abigail Adams settled into their first home. It was a small house (they called it a cottage) that adjoined the main building of the Adams homestead in Braintree. Abigail occupied herself with setting up housekeeping, and John found that his law practice was busier than before, because many friends and connections of the Quincy family now gave him their business. The Adamses found time, however, to visit often at Mount Wollaston, where John talked politics with "Grandfather" Colonel John Quincy. The newlyweds were busy and happy, and as Adams threw himself into day-to-day life, he abandoned his diary for a while.

He resumed writing in his diary in 1765, when he had several momentous things to record. So exciting was 1765 that Adams later called his 30th year "the most remarkable year of my life."

PUBLISHING AND PATRIOTISM

The "remarkable year" began with the publication of chapters from a book Adams was writing called *A Dissertation on Canon and Feudal Law.* Parts of it were published in installments in newspapers in America and England. It was a detailed study of the legal rights of churches and governments, and it established Adams as an important thinker. It also showed signs of his growing love of America and his desire to safeguard American liberty.

In the *Dissertation,* Adams argued their long history of conquest and oppression had burdened the European nations with tyranny. That is, people's liberties were suppressed by the powers of kings and churches. Such tyranny, he said, was not acceptable in America. The colonies had been founded for the special purpose of religious liberty, and political liberty must accompany it. But Adams did not suggest that America should become independent. He felt that the American colonies were very much a part of England. He just wanted the American people to enjoy the same rights and liberties that Englishmen everywhere should have: freedom from unfair taxation and permission to choose their own governors.

Although Adams' writings did not call for a break with England, there were many people in America who had grown impatient with England's tight hold on her colonies. Some of them agreed with Adams that the rules governing the colonies should be changed, but others wanted complete independence. These people approved of Adams' accusation of tyranny in his *Dissertation,* and they began to think of him as an American patriot.

Taxation Without Representation

Then, while Adams was finishing the *Dissertation,* an event occurred that forced Americans to take sides for or against the English government. That event was the Stamp Act of 1765. It was an attempt by the English to raise money by requiring the American colonists to buy stamps for many different purposes, including the sale and purchase of property, business transactions, and the registration of births, weddings, and deaths. The cost of the stamps was really a new tax to be paid to England—where the colonists had no one to speak for them in the Parliament.

Samuel Adams, John Adams' cousin, was a well-known Boston patriot who helped engineer the Boston Tea Party. Like John Adams, Samuel Adams signed the Declaration of Independence. (Library of Congress.)

Many Americans were outraged at England's latest oppression. The colonies took up the cry: "No taxation without representation!" Adams was caught up in the excitement. He rewrote the last installment of the *Dissertation* to include a section about the unfairness of the Stamp Act. He was also chosen to write the Braintree Instructions, a statement that set forth the town's opposition to the act. And he wrote in his diary that the Stamp Act was an "enormous engine, fabricated by the British Parliament, for battering down all the rights and liberties of America." But none of the opposition to the Stamp Act kept it from becoming law. However, his writings about the act did have the effect of grouping Adams with the patriot movement, which included such men as Benjamin Edes, printer of the Boston *Gazette,* and Samuel Adams, John's cousin.

A GROWING FAMILY AND CAREER

Another momentous event that occurred in 1765 was the birth of John and Abigail's first child on July 14. They named her Abigail Amelia Adams. Nearly two years later, on July 11, 1767, their second child was born. He was named John Quincy Adams, in honor of Abigail's grandfather, the old colonel.

During the 1760s, Adams' law business continued to prosper. Although he had to work hard and certainly never made a fortune, he was able to pay his bills and keep his growing family comfortable: Susanna Adams was born in 1768, Charles Adams in 1770, and Thomas Boylston Adams in 1772.

Around 1768, Adams entered the most active period of his law career. He made frequent journeys on horseback to attend sessions in the circuit courts of the area and was often away from home for a week or longer. Abigail calmly took charge of running the farm with the help of one or two servants. In the late 1760s, the Adamses moved into a small house in Boston.

Adams' most prestigious client was the Kennebeck Company of Maine, which paid him well to come to Maine regularly to handle the company's legal affairs. One of the company's businesses was logging in the forests of Maine and New Hampshire. Because tall, straight trees were much in demand as masts for ships, the British had made a rule that a certain number of such "mast" trees had to be turned over to the government. The company and its lawyer were always arguing with British representatives over who owned the trees. By coincidence, one of these representatives was John Wentworth, the Royal Governor of New Hampshire and Surveyor of the King's Woods, who was an old classmate of Adams' from Harvard. Although the two engaged in many legal battles over the "mast" rights, there is no sign that their battles were ever unfriendly.

Busy as he was, Adams still found time to write in his diary. Occasionally he returned to the subject of ambition that had perplexed him years before: "Am I grasping at money, or scheming for power?" he demanded of himself. "Am I planning the illustration [fame] of my family or the welfare of my country? These are great questions."

Neither could he keep politics out of his thoughts. Although he repeatedly wrote and said that he no longer cared for "newspaper politics," and that he was going to devote himself to his law practice, Adams continued to read the newspapers and to follow current events closely. He became caught up in politics again in 1770, when he took part in a sensational legal case.

A Test of Courage and Conscience

British soldiers had been sent to Boston and other cities in the colonies in the late 1760s, even though the French and Indian War was long over. Although the governors of the colonies explained that the troops were there only to discourage

*In 1770, British troops fired on civilians in the notorious
"Boston Massacre." Adams felt that the hated British deserved
a fair trial and courageously helped defend them. This act won
the respect of most of his fellow colonists. (Library of
Congress.)*

France or any other nation from making war on the colonies, the colonists suspected that the real reason for their presence was to keep them in line. The Americans resented the troops, and several disputes broke out between the soldiers and the colonists. The most notorious was the Boston Massacre.

On the night of March 5, 1770, British troops fired into a crowd of citizens. The soldiers were to be tried for murder. Adams agreed to help defend them, even though he hated what they had done, because he believed that everyone was entitled to a fair trial under the law.

The trial dragged on until December and cost Adams much labor and well-being. He made a number of powerful speeches upholding the dignity of the law, and he wrote countless articles and legal statements. The outcome was something of a success for Adams, for the soldiers were not hanged. And Adams' decision to defend the British soldiers did not cost him much popularity among the anti-British colonists. Most of them regarded him as a courageous man of conscience.

Despite his personal victory in the case, Adams was exhausted at the end of 1770. He was now 35 years old, considered middle-aged for the 18th century, and he felt that his health had been damaged by the "bad air" and noise of Boston. He returned with Abigail and the children to the family farm in Braintree. He felt the need for solitude and time to think, so he took a long horseback ride into the Connecticut River Valley, stopping at a place called Stafford Springs to drink the mineral water, which was believed to be good for one's health.

When Adams returned to Braintree, feeling rested and refreshed, he vowed once again to leave politics alone, to work in his practice, and to spend time with his family and his farm. For these reasons, he did not take part in some of the patriotic activities of the early 1770s, such as the Boston Committee of Correspondence organized by his cousin Samuel.

Although Adams did not take part in the Boston Tea Party of 1773, he was soon caught up in the revolutionary movement that swept through the colonies after the Bostonians threw 342 chests of tea into Boston Harbor rather than pay British taxes on them. (Library of Congress.)

By 1773, however, Adams' old political interests were stirring again. He exchanged bitter words with Thomas Hutchinson, the British-appointed governor of Massachusetts, over which had more authority: the English parliament or the Massachusetts Colony General Court. Of course, he was unable to convince Hutchinson, whom he always regarded as an enemy, that the local court outranked the Parliament.

Tea and Taxes

In December of 1773, there occurred what Adams called a "magnificent" event: the Boston Tea Party. Patriots refused to pay taxes on tea imported from England and dumped tons of it into the Boston harbor. Adams thought that this was a wonderful gesture against tyranny and illegal taxation. Although he played no part in the event, his cousin Samuel was one of those who helped arrange it.

As Adams feared, the British retaliated for the Boston Tea Party. The port of Boston was closed and the colonists were told to pay for the tea. New acts were introduced. The Regulating Act made the Massachusetts colony's government even more oppressive, and the Quebec Act was an attempt to make the Canadian province as big and important as the American colonies. The colonists were furious at these reprisals. From this point on, the tide of events moved even more swiftly toward revolution and independence. John Adams knew that he had to be a part of these stirring events. His background of service to the community, his learning, and his passionate belief in the importance of good government — all led him toward patriotism, even though he hated war.

THE CONTINENTAL CONGRESS

In the summer of 1774, Adams was asked to be one of four representatives from Massachusetts at a meeting, or "congress," of important men from all the colonies (Samuel Adams

also represented Massachusetts). The task of these representatives was to convince the people of the other colonies that
the crisis in Boston should concern all Americans.

The meeting was to be held in Philadelphia. Adams' diary
gives a detailed account of his journey. He reported that many
people along the way, including Silas Deane in Connecticut,
who would figure again in Adams' life several years later, gave
him encouragement. He also noted such points as the ex-
cellence of Philadelphia beer and the looser manners and
morals of the Philadelphians.

The representatives who gathered in Philadelphia in 1774
were far from united on the questions of what to do and how
to proceed. They ranged from "moderates," who wanted the
rights of Americans to be respected *within* the British Empire, to "radicals," who wanted to set up an ideal new government separate from England (this would mean, of course, a
war for independence). Some of the representatives were
Loyalists, who considered themselves Englishmen and felt
loyalty to the king; others, including Adams, were Whigs,
who felt that the colonies should govern themselves, even if
they remained associated with the Empire.

One of the acts of the First Continental Congress was
the drawing up of a petition to George III of England, the
"Most Gracious Sovereign," pleading for greater liberty. The
representatives also drew up a list of rights and grievances
based on English law and the colonial charters. Finally, they
passed what was called the Association (because the Congress was not a law-making body, they couldn't call it a law).
It was an order forbidding the colonists to have any trade or
social dealings with the British.

The Association was to make life miserable for
moderates and Loyalists during the following year. Committees of Whigs bustled about in every city, town, and village,
lecturing their fellow colonists against such luxuries as horse-

racing or ballroom dancing. Anyone suspected of violating the Association was reported in the newspapers. In some cases, violators were tarred and feathered or otherwise punished by vigilante committees. A prominent clergyman, Bishop Seabury, wrote that he would rather be enslaved by a king than by a bunch of self-important Whig Committeemen, whom he said were like rats and vermin.

When the Congress ended in October of 1774, Adams returned to Braintree, happy in the belief that at last he was taking part in great events. He found further patriotic work to do in Massachusetts. One of the newspapers was running a series of articles by an anonymous Loyalist, or Tory, who signed himself "Massachusettensis." The articles were witty, intelligent, and well-written. Adams saw that they might very well make friends for the Tory cause, so he decided to answer these articles on behalf of the Whigs. His essays, for which he used the pen name "Novanglus," soon appeared. The two anonymous writers carried on a lively exchange of opinions for several months. Then, as Adams wrote later, "the battle of Lexington on the 19th of April [1775] changed the instruments of warfare from the pen to the sword."

After years of growing discontent with British rule on the part of the colonists, fighting had at last broken out. A month later, the Second Continental Congress met in Philadelphia. Although Adams' diary is less revealing about the events of 1775 than it had been for the previous year, he did keep a careful record of expenses and worried about money and his health (Philadelphia, like so many places he was to visit, had "bad air").

Bad Press, Good Press

The 1775 Congress was especially difficult for Adams because of a humiliating incident. He had written a letter that rashly accused John Dickinson, a very moderate Whig, of trying to come to peace terms with the British. The letter, in which Adams spoke of Dickinson in unnecessarily rude terms, was intercepted by the British and published throughout the colonies. Dickinson was furious, the British were both angry and amused, and Adams realized that he looked like a hot-headed, indiscreet fool. He vowed in his diary to exercise greater prudence in the future—but lack of judgment, especially when it came to criticizing the faults of others, was always to cause trouble for him.

Early in 1776, Tom Paine's famous book, *Common Sense,* was published in the colonies. Many people believed that this attack on the British monarchy had really been written by John Adams. But Adams felt that Paine was a "tearer down" of government. He wanted to be a "builder up," so he published *Thoughts on Government* that same year. This book was the result of his lengthy study and thought about the science of government.

Adams hoped that the *Thoughts* would help some of the colonies design their new state constitutions, as indeed it did. Several of the principles that form the basis of American government were set forth in this book by Adams, including the checks-and-balances system of dividing power between the executive, legislative, and judiciary branches of government and the bicameral (two-chambered) legislature, in which each house (senate and representatives) has the power to hold back or balance the other.

Like all of the delegates to the Continental Congress, Adams worked long and hard on many committees, for almost no pay. At the same time, he was horrified by the news from home. An epidemic had swept through eastern Massachusetts, killing Abigail's mother and Adams' younger brother, Elihu. In the hope of avoiding the illness, Abigail even underwent the dreaded pox inoculation.

But his personal troubles never kept John Adams from

This engraving of the signing of the Declaration of Independence is copied from a famous painting by John Trumbull, the so-called "Patriot Artist," whose works are a valuable record of America's early history. Adams is the figure on the left of the group standing in the center. (Library of Congress.)

fulfilling his public duty. By the summer of 1776, he was ready to make his greatest contribution to American liberty.

THE ATLAS OF INDEPENDENCE

In ancient mythology, Atlas is the strong man who bears the world on his back. Even when he is bent almost double by the immense burden, Atlas never fails and the earth never falls. Over the centuries, the name "Atlas" came to mean anyone who planted his feet, stood steadfast, and shouldered a heavy burden.

Adams was appointed by the second Continental Congress to serve on a committee that was to draw up a formal Declaration of Independence. The document that resulted—the one that Americans celebrate every July 4th—was largely the work of Thomas Jefferson of Virginia, whose later political life was to be closely connected with Adams'. The job fell to Jefferson because he had the reputation of being a good writer, and the Declaration is a brilliant piece of writing. But another important job—that of defending the Declaration before the Congress—fell to Adams, who had a reputation of being a good public speaker.

Historians have always regretted that there is no record of Adams' speeches in defense of the Declaration of Independence. We know that as many as one-third of the delegates to the Congress did not agree with the Declaration's principles or its wording, yet Adams defeated all their objections. His stirring speeches carried the day, and the Declaration of Independence, with its call for "life, liberty, and the pursuit of happiness," became one of the most important documents in history.

Three of the delegates later commented that Adams had been like an Atlas in his strength on the floor of the Con-

Adams, on the left, was one of a committee sent by Congress to negotiate with England's representative, Lord Howe, in September of 1776 on Staten Island. The peace talks failed, and the War of Independence followed. (Library of Congress.)

gress. One man who used the expression was Jefferson. Although he and Adams were later to become enemies, and then friends again in old age, Jefferson never forgot that he had called Adams "the Atlas of Independence." Without Adams' brilliant speeches, Jefferson's famous document might have ended up in the waste-paper basket.

Adams himself had mixed feelings about Jefferson. While he admired the Virginian's wit and intelligence, he felt that Jefferson's fame was overblown. Many years later, he wrote to his friend, Dr. Benjamin Rush, that "Jefferson ran away with all the stage effect" and "all the glory." Adams also felt a little bitter that the world overlooked his own contributions to the Declaration of Rights, which had been produced by the 1774 Congress and quickly forgotten.

For the next year, Adams continued to serve his newborn country in Philadelphia, its first capital. He did great quantities of committee work and paperwork, including writing hundreds of letters, without the help of a secretary. He also headed the Congressional Board of War. One of his acts was to recommend George Washington as commander-in-chief of the Continental Army. By doing so, he made an enemy of an old friend and client, John Hancock, who had wanted the position for himself. But John Adams always believed in doing what he thought was right, even if it meant stepping on a few toes.

In November of 1777, at age 42, Adams left Philadelphia for his home in Braintree. He had done his best to make use of his talents and learning in the highest service he knew — service to one's country — and now he planned to return to his family, his law practice, and his farm. But the familiar pattern of a brief retirement, followed by a new call to service, was about to repeat itself. This time, the call would take Adams across the Atlantic Ocean.

Chapter 5

The Ambassador

The next stage of his public career would be one of the most difficult periods of Adams' life. It consisted of frustration, failure, long separations from Abigail, and illness—even a type of nervous breakdown. Yet the years between 1779 and 1788 would contain some triumphs, too.

With the Revolutionary War now well under way, America's leaders began to concern themselves with international diplomacy. As a new nation, the United States would have to develop relationships with other countries. The sooner she did so, the better, because America needed all the help she could get in her struggle against the British. The first nation to side with the United States was France. The French were willing to help the American patriots with money and supplies, not so much for the sake of America as a way to strike back at England, France's old enemy.

When war broke out, travel across the Atlantic became dangerous for Americans, who were likely to be captured as prisoners of war or even spies by the British. For this reason, the Continental Congress appointed two men who were already in Europe at the time to serve as commissioners to the French court. They were Arthur Lee of Virginia and Silas Deane of Connecticut. In addition, Dr. Benjamin Franklin, the fiery old patriot, risked the sea voyage to France to join them. This three-member commission was supposed to make political and trade treaties, or agreements, with France.

For various reasons, the Congress suspected that Deane was not keeping accurate accounts of the money spent in France on behalf of the American government. Some thought he was actually dishonest; others accused him of merely hoping to profit from the revolution. Finally, the Congress decided to replace him. Their choice for the replacement was John Adams.

Adams had earned a reputation for integrity. In fact, some people called him "Honest John Adams." And because he had served on a congressional committee in 1776 to draw up a model of a treaty for use in future foreign affairs, he had some experience for the job. He seemed like the perfect choice. The fact that he was sometimes temperamental and hard to get along with, or that he did not have much of a reputation for tactful, diplomatic behavior, did not seem to matter very much.

Thus it was that only a few months after he had returned again to his beloved Braintree to settle down, Adams was asked to go to France. Tired as he was, he felt he could not refuse this request for his services. At first he hoped to take Abigail and the children with him, as he realized that he would be gone for some time, perhaps a year. He sent out urgent bills to all of the clients who owed him money, hoping to raise the funds to pay for his family's passage. But when he and Abigail counted up the results, they were forced to admit that there simply wasn't enough money. So Adams set off in 1778 with only his oldest son, John Quincy (called "Johnny" by the family), as company.

A STRANGE NEW LAND

The trials and terrors of the voyage—first being chased by British warships and then lost in a fearful storm—were all forgotten as soon as the Adamses landed at Bordeaux. For all his reading and studying, Adams was a simple man from a farming background who had traveled little. The sophistication and luxury of the French court both fascinated him and troubled his strict Puritan spirit.

First, there was the food. While still in the Bordeaux harbor, Adams ate dinner aboard a French cruiser and later wrote in his diary that the liver in a rich sauce and the dessert of juicy raisins were the best meal he had ever had. Although he would eventually complain that the rich French food (along with the bad air, of course) had ruined his health, in the beginning Adams enjoyed it very much.

Then there were the amusements. Adams loved going to the theater—although he tried to pass this pleasure off as studying the language by taking the scripts of the plays with him. He wrote with pleased excitement about the cafes, the beautiful buildings, and the shops of Paris.

Finally, there were the French people. Adams was sometimes shocked and always fascinated by the worldly, pleasure-loving French. He wrote with disapproval that at the home of a Madame Brillon, where Franklin took him to dine, dinner guests shared the table with both Madame Brillon's lover and her husband's mistress—and yet he continued to dine there.

He recorded many experiences that show how the Puritan in him was both attracted to and disgusted by French behavior. In one of these episodes, he sat at dinner next to an attractive and witty woman named Madame de Texel. She startled Adams by saying: "Mr. Adams, by your name I conclude you are descended from the first man and woman, and probably in your family may be preserved the tradition which may resolve a difficulty I never could explain. I never could understand how the first couple found out the art of lying together?"

Adams blushed with distress. He had never heard a woman speak so bluntly of personal matters. But he tried to remain composed and answered her laboriously and scientifically through a translator: "There was a physical quality in us resembling the power of electricity or of the magnet, by which when a pair approached withing striking distance they flew together like the needle to the pole [of a compass] or like two objects in electric experiments."

"Well," she replied with a smile, "I know not how it was, but this I know: it is a very happy shock!"

Despite this and other unnerving encounters, Adams soon felt comfortable enough in France. He was determined, though, not to run the risk of appearing greedy, like Deane. As a result, he lived as cheaply as he could, borrowing Franklin's carriage or walking whenever possible instead of renting a carriage of his own. His first task was to unscramble the commission's tangled account books. Once that had been done, he looked about him for the next duty. It was at this point that his troubles began.

Disappointments and Disillusionment

Adams suffered two disappointments in his commission. One was the discovery that, unknown to him, Franklin and Lee had successfully completed an alliance with France before Adams arrived. The news of the alliance had not reached America before Adams left for France. When he announced that he was ready to begin work on the treaty, Adams learned from Franklin and others that the job was almost complete. In other words, Adams had left his home and family and risked a dangerous sea voyage only to find that he wasn't needed, after all. For someone who took great pride in his usefulness and sense of duty, this was a crushing blow. He had nothing to do but wait around France for orders from the Congress to come home.

In the meantime, Adams tried to get involved in some of the final stages of making the treaty. There were many details to be ironed out, and he itched to do his share of the ironing. But at this point, he suffered his second disappointment. He was politely shut out of the negotiations, and he was certain that Ben Franklin was responsible.

Adams accused Franklin of trying to grab all the credit for French affairs. In response, Franklin claimed that Adams set about the matter clumsily and failed to win the trust of the Count of Vergennes, who was France's foreign minister. Vergennes had the notion that Adams was not totally anti-British, perhaps because Adams was a moderate Whig and not a radical. As a result, Vergennes tended to dismiss Adams. Vergennes, in turn, was just the type of polished, old-world European courtier who made Adams uneasy and distrustful; Adams also resented Franklin's ease and friendliness with men like Vergennes. To top it all off, Adams described Franklin as a "moral disgrace" because of his well-known fondness for the ladies. In short, before long Adams and Franklin detested each other.

As soon as Adams received word from the Congress that his appointment to the commission was ended, he rushed to the port of Nantes, eager to put the frustration of his mission behind him and return home. Here, yet another disappointment awaited him. Although Adams arrived in Nantes in March of 1779, he was not able to leave until June.

Originally, Adams was to sail for the United States on an American ship, the *Alliance,* commanded by a Captain Landais. For more than a month, from March 12 until April 28, he and Johnny lived in the cramped quarters of a ship's cabin while they waited for the captain to receive his sailing orders. Then Adams received a letter from Franklin, transferring him to a French ship, the *La Sensible.* He was to wait aboard the *Sensible* until the new French ambassador to the United States arrived in Nantes, then Adams and the ambassador would make the voyage together.

Impatient and ill, Adams transferred to the *Sensible*. To his fury, however, the French ambassador didn't arrive in Nantes until June 11. A week later, the *Sensible* finally set sail.

Adams brooded a great deal over the delay and discourtesy of his departure. He suspected that Franklin had prevented him from sailing on the *Alliance* because Franklin's friend, John Paul Jones, wanted to add the ship to his fleet in order to make himself a commodore. This suspicion made sense to Adams because Jones and he had never been friendly; Jones sarcastically referred to Adams as "Mr. Roundface," and Adams resented it.

The de-commissioned commissioner never got to the bottom of the Nantes business. He was sick at heart about his failure to be useful on the commission, and he was glad to be going home. But his distrust and dislike of Franklin remained strong. Unfortunately, he was about to tangle with the wily old doctor for a second time.

THE PEACE-MAKER

Adams arrived in Boston in August of 1779. He settled in for a long visit with Abigail and the children, but within a few weeks he was elected to represent Braintree at the Massachusetts constitutional convention, to draw up the state constitution. This was a duty that was also a pleasure, because Adams had always taken just as much interest in state and local affairs as in national and international ones. He also had a special interest in constitutions and theories of government, and he hoped to be able to put some of what he had written in *Thoughts on Government* into the Massachusetts constitution.

He had better success in Cambridge, the site of the convention, than he had in France. Today, Adams is recognized as the chief designer of the Massachusetts constitution. It used his system of checks and balances and made sure that the three branches of government — legislative, executive, and judiciary — remained independent from one another, as he had insisted.

Even before the people of Massachusetts voted to accept the new constitution, Adams set off on still another mission for his country. He was asked to return to France to begin preparations for a peace treaty with England. Because Adams knew how important such a treaty could be, and because he wanted to prove himself after the "failure" of his first mission to France, he did not hesitate to say yes.

Once again Adams made the perilous winter crossing, this time traveling in the familiar *Sensible*. With him were a secretary and a servant (a young family friend whose parents wanted him to see Europe), his friend Francis Dana (who had received a congressional appointment to France), Dana's secretary, and Adams' two oldest sons, John Quincy and his nine-year-old brother Charles. This time Johnny had wanted to stay home, but his father insisted that the trip would give him valuable opportunities for learning.

This time the ocean crossing was uneventful, except that a minor leak in the ship forced them to land at Port Ferrol, Spain. But from then on, the party encountered a series of difficulties and discomforts. They had to make an overland journey to Paris, crossing rugged mountains on the way, in the dead of winter. Traveling by mule, horseback, and broken-down carriage, they finally reached Paris in February of 1780. Nearly everyone was sick. Adams alone stayed healthy. This may seem surprising, given Adams' fussiness about his health. However, inactivity, feelings of uselessness, and long stretches of city life seem to have made him sick. Vigorous outdoor adventures in midwinter probably suited him very well.

To his dismay, Adams found that diplomatic conditions in France were even worse than when he had left. His old enemy, Ben Franklin, seemed to be firmly in control of all dealings between the French and the Americans.

Vergennes and the French, it appeared, were angry that the United States might even consider making peace with England. At the same time, France and Spain were allies. Spain wanted to seize the Rock of Gibraltar, which was controlled by England. This would mean war between Spain and England, and France's treaty with Spain meant that France would have to join in the war against England. For this reason, Vergennes wanted England and the United States to remain at war: the more England worried about America, the less strength it could throw against France.

A New Diplomacy

All of these complicated considerations were distasteful to Adams. He wanted to practice a new, blunt kind of American diplomacy, which he called "shirt-sleeve" diplomacy. Franklin, however, rejected his efforts. Adams then decided that he could accomplish nothing in France, and he and his sons went to Holland in July. Adams hoped that he could use Holland as a base from which to approach England about treaty negotiations.

This plan backfired badly when, soon after Adams arrived in Holland, the Dutch and English went to war. Henry Laurens, an American who had served as president of one of the Continental Congresses, had been the United States diplomat in Holland. Unfortunately, he was in England when the war broke out. The British promptly threw him into the Tower of London, where he languished for months, writing long letters of complaint home to the United States. So Adams decided to take Laurens' place in Amsterdam. He realized that he couldn't make any progress on diplomatic relations with England for the time being, but he hoped to get somewhere with the Dutch.

As it turned out, Adams proved to be a successful diplomat in Amsterdam, which was then the political center of Holland. He eventually negotiated a treaty in which Holland recognized the independence of the United States. He also managed to get a loan for the new nation from the Dutch banks. These efforts took time, however—much more time than he had expected. The treaty and the loan were not finalized until 1782.

Meanwhile, during all of 1781, Adams had little to do but wait in Holland, arguing his case with any Dutch diplomat or banker he could corner. It was a long, lonely year for him. John Quincy wanted a change, so his father allowed him to go to Russia with Francis Dana. Charley then grew homesick, so he was permitted to return home. Adams wished he could return home as well, and several times wrote to Abigail to expect him, but he was never able to finish up his business. She offered to join him in Holland, but he was afraid that by the time she arrived, he would be ready to leave. So their separation continued. And, as usual, inactivity, frustration, and city life had a poor effect on Adams' health. He had a serious spell of illness; this time he blamed it on bad water, instead of air. After all, he was in Holland, a country built on water.

The year of 1782 saw a great improvement. Not only did Adams finally conclude his long-awaited treaty and loan with the Dutch, but a fine, small hotel was purchased by the United States and turned into the American legation (embassy building) in Amsterdam. Best of all, the British government changed in the middle of the year.

A new prime minister took office in England in July. Because it was fearful of conflicts that might break out in Europe at any moment, the new English government decided to cut its losses and make peace with the Americans—even recognizing their independence, if there was no other way. At long last, it looked like Adams would be able to get to work on his original goal: a peace treaty with England.

Fears and Folly

But his instructions from Congress did not give Adams sole power to negotiate with the British. The treaty was to be the work of all five of the American ambassadors who were then in Europe: Adams, Franklin, John Jay (who had been in Madrid), Henry Laurens (released from his imprisonment in the Tower), and Thomas Jefferson (a new arrival). As soon as work on the treaty got under way, Adams' anxiety grew. He suspected the others, especially Franklin, of keeping him in the dark and of being too afraid of offending France. He also feared that the British would take advantage of disagreements among the American negotiating team in order to weaken the treaty.

The site of the treaty negotiations was Paris. In spite of Adams' fears, all went smoothly. Most of the details of the treaty had been worked out by November of 1782. Adams' major contribution, and one of which he remained proud to the end of his days, was the clause that gave Americans the freedom to fish in the rich fishing-grounds off Newfoundland in the North Atlantic. Adams even had a family seal designed bearing a picture of a fish and the motto "We will fish and hunt as heretofore." It is not recorded that he ever used the seal.

Although the treaty negotiations had gone smoothly, both England and the United States dragged their feet over the process of ratifying (approving) the treaty. Ratification took almost a year, from November of 1782 to September of 1783. This year of waiting, without permission to come home but without anything to do, was one of the worst years in Adams' life.

He wrote to Abigail that he was obsessed with nervous, fidgeting behavior. He described "sharp, fiery humors [possibly boils] that break out in the back of my neck and other parts of me and plague me as much as the uncertainty which I am in of my future destination." Some of Adams'

Gilbert Stuart painted this portrait of Abigail Adams to accompany that of her husband. Although her lace cap and shawl were probably costly, she usually dressed in simple, plain clothes. (Library of Congress.)

behavior at this time gave rise to a reputation of mental instability that he was never to shake. He gossiped irresponsibly and childishly about Franklin, Vergennes, and other people—who soon heard of it and resented it. He also hinted to everyone, not very subtly, that he deserved the post of first ambassador to England.

In a costly move, he sent a copy of his diary of the peace negotiations to a member of Congress, with instructions to read it aloud. Although he intended the members of Congress to be impressed with his shrewdness at the bargaining table, the result was not what he had hoped for. In fact, the listeners never even reached the part of the diary that told of the negotiations. The entire Congress broke into scornful laughter at a long passage in which Adams described how well Vergennes had treated him one day when he took him to lunch at the Palace of Versailles. Adams' childish and vain account of how Vergennes had bowed to him and handed him a piece of cake made the Massachusetts diplomat look like a silly oaf. The reader stopped when the laughter broke out, but the damage was done. Hereafter, some people were to think of Adams as an honest man but one who was also naive and vain.

The most devastating comment about Adams' behavior during this period—when he may very well have undergone a minor nervous breakdown from loneliness, overwork, and worry—came from Franklin. He wrote to Congress that he believed Adams "means well for his country, is always an honest man, sometimes a wise one, but sometimes, and in some things, absolutely out of his senses." To the annoyance of Adams and Abigail, the remark was often repeated and became famous.

To Adams' relief, his wife and daughter Abigail (called Nabby like her mother) joined him in Europe in 1784, and John Quincy returned from St. Petersburg, Russia. They settled in a small villa in Auteuil, a few miles outside Paris. They were to live there for a year while John waited to see whether he would receive an ambassadorial post. It was a restful, happy time in Adams' life. The Adamses went out very little: Abigail went to the opera from time to time, and John took daily walks in the nearby Bois de Boulogne, a large, forested park.

Young Nabby had been brought to France by her parents in the hope that she would give up a love affair they disapproved of. Adams and Abigail did not want to be tyrannical parents. They did not order Nabby to stop seeing young Royall Tyler of Braintree, even though they thought he was flighty and shallow. Instead, they took her to Europe and kept her there until her romance with young Tyler had died. By a strange coincidence, Tyler had once owned a large house in Braintree that Adams had recently bought to live in when he returned from Europe. That same house, now in Quincy, Massachusetts, is the Adams National Historical Site.

AMBASSADORSHIP AND WRITING

In 1785, Adams received his wish: he was made the first American ambassador to England. He, Abigail, and Nabby left France for the American legation in Grosvenor Square, London.

In later years, Adams made it plain that he had not especially enjoyed his stay in London. He complained that the British were cold, formally polite, and reserved. Such behavior is understandable, considering that the two countries had just finished fighting a bitter war, but Adams disliked it anyway. He and Abigail had their greatest pleasure on outings into the beautiful English countryside. One trip they particularly enjoyed was a visit to Shakespeare's home at Stratford-on-Avon. Adams also made two trips to Holland, one of which was to settle the details of a new loan to the United States.

The Adamses were in England for four years. There was little ambassadorial business, and in truth Adams found the time to pass slowly. He wrote a three-volume work called *Defence of the Constitutions of the Government of the United States of America.* It is a long, rambling work that contains countless examples of the strengths and weaknesses of different types of governments, drawn from all periods of history. Some of Adams' statements in the *Defence* were taken by his enemies to mean that he approved of aristocrats and kings, and quotes from the work would later pop up to haunt him during his presidency.

Perhaps the most important event of their stay in England was Nabby's marriage to Colonel William Smith, an assistant at the legation. Her first child, and John and Abigail's first grandchild, was born in London. Although Nabby's parents had approved of the dashing Smith, he turned out to be a constant worry. He never made enough money to support his grand schemes, and he and Nabby had many personal problems. (Ironically, Royall Tyler, whom Nabby's parents had thought was a ne'er-do-well, turned out to be a successful playwright and the chief justice of the state of Vermont.)

In 1788, Adams' appointment as ambassador to England drew to a close. He was ready and eager to return to the United States after nearly a decade spent in France, Holland, and England. He and Abigail set sail for home in the summer of 1788, looking forward to their new house in Quincy (the part of Braintree that would eventually become a town of its own). John was now 53 and Abigail was 44. Both of them believed that all that lay ahead was a comfortable, well-earned retirement.

Chapter 6

The Vice-President

A dams returned to the United States on the eve of a great experiment. A new form of government was about to begin.

During Adams' last year in Britain, the Continental Congress had met for the last time in Philadelphia to draw up a national constitution for the United States. Adams must have been sorry that he wasn't part of the Constitutional Convention, as it was called. He firmly believed that the United States needed a strong constitutional foundation in order to survive. But he took some satisfaction in knowing that the first volume of his *Defence of the Constitutions* had arrived in Philadelphia in time to remind the delegates of his views.

When the work of the Constitutional Convention was done, Adams approved of it. It called for a central, or federal, government to bind the governments of the states together. It also included the system of checks and balances, the bicameral legislature, and the separation of powers that Adams felt were important. Now the nation was getting ready to put its new constitution into practice by electing its first President.

RETURN AND RECOGNITION

To his pleased surprise, Adams found upon his return home that he was regarded as an important public figure. His four years in England, during which he had been able to accomplish little real work, had left him feeling uncertain of his value to his country. But Congress publicly thanked him for his "patriotism, perseverance, integrity, and diligence," and at last he felt that his worth had been recongized. Now, just when he thought his life's work was over, he began to receive offers of new positions.

At first, during the autumn of 1788, Adams concentrated on domestic matters. He and Abigail moved into their new house in Quincy. Although it was larger than the old Adams' family house, the rooms were still small and low-ceilinged; Abigail called it a "wren's nest." But Adams liked the brook that ran past the new house. He walked along it every day, and he took up his old habit of fishing.

Everyone in the United States felt the great shortage of money during the years after the war. Like all farmers, Adams worried about his finances and grumbled that he didn't have enough cash. At this time, politicians made little or no money from their public services, and all of them were expected to have other sources of income. But he threw himself with delight into another of his old pleasures, farm work. He surveyed his estate, made plans for its future, and tackled all the chores with great energy. Abigail did the same, taking responsibility for the dairy. She often laughingly described herself during the coming years as a "dairy-maid."

Adams also was pleased to be near his son John Quincy again. Like his father, John Quincy had gone to Harvard and then decided to study law. Just as his father had studied with "Old Put," young John was now studying in the office of Theophilus Parsons, in Newburyport, Massachusetts. John Quincy often visited his father. On one visit, he found Adams busy with a necessary farm chore, so he rolled up his shirtsleeves and helped his father pitch manure (used as fertilizer) over the gardens. During one of these visits, Adams suggested to John Quincy that the two of them start a father-and-son law practice, but it was not to be. By the time John Quincy was ready to go into practice, Adams had once more shouldered the burden of public service.

As soon as Adams returned to the United States, in fact, he was elected a representative to the final session of the Continental Congress. He never took his seat there because that congress was breaking up to make way for the new congress that would be elected under the Constitution. Then Adams was approached about being governor of Massachusetts, or perhaps a senator. In past years, he had devoted himself energetically to serving his state, but now he felt that the new experiment in federal government was much more significant. If he came back into politics at all, he decided, it would have to be in a position of national importance. He began to think about the coming election.

THE FIRST ELECTION

From the start, the United States has used an electoral system to choose its high officers – although details of the system have changed from time to time. Voters select the candidates of their choice, but the actual election of the President is done by the electoral college (a group of people from each state who cast their states' electoral votes). Although the electors are expected to follow the pattern of the people's votes, they do not always do so. In fact, one of the age-old debates about the American form of government concerns the electoral college: Who really elects the president? Is it the people, or the electors?

Electoral College Assembled

Back in 1788, no one was really sure that the system would work, but everyone was eager to try the democratic experiment. The states assembled an electoral college. The number of electors allowed to each state was based on its population. Various means were used to select the electors. In some states, they were elected by the state legislatures. In others, they were appointed by the governors. Some states used a combination of these methods. The result was a group of 69 men who were responsible for electing the first President and Vice-President of the United States. Each elector had two votes, one for President and one for Vice-President.

The "candidates" of 1788 were quite different from those of the 20th century. First, they did not belong to political parties (the party system did not develop until a few years later, during Adams' years as Vice-President and President, in fact). Secondly, the candidates did not campaign for votes. Once they agreed to run for office, their names were simply included in the list given to the electors. And candidates did not run for the office of President or Vice-President. They simply ran for office, and the electors decided who would be President and who would be Vice-President.

Nearly everyone expected George Washington, the hero of the Revolutionary War, to be the first President. Adams knew this. In fact, he felt that Washington should be President as he (Adams) did not think he could be elected. He was confident, though, that he would be Vice-President, so he decided to run.

The Vote and The Outcome

The electors cast their momentous votes in November of 1788. The first vote was unanimous. As had been expected, all 69 of the electors cast their first votes for George Washington. But when it came time for the second vote, Adams' troubles began.

Adams probably did not expect to receive all 69 votes. After all, if both votes had been unanimous, how would the electors have chosen one of the two men for President? But

Who Really Elects the President?

We think of the United States as a democracy whose leaders are chosen by its citizens through popular elections (one vote for each person qualified to vote). In reality, though, the President and Vice-President are elected by a little-understood group called the electoral college. The choices made by the electoral college are *usually* the same as the choices made by the people at large—but not always. It has even happened that the electoral college has elected a President who did not receive a majority of the popular vote.

The electoral college was established under Article II, Section I, of the Constitution. In Adams' time, each state chose a number of electors equal to the total number of its senators and representatives. The method by which the electors were chosen varied from state to state. In some states, the electors were chosen by the people and were likely to represent the popular views. In other states, however, the electors represented the government in power and were not bound to follow popular opinion.

At the time Adams ran for President, in 1796 and again in 1800, each elector had two votes (but could not cast both for the same person). The electors met and cast their votes in a single, large election. Whoever got the largest number of votes was President; whoever got the second largest number was Vice-President. If there was a tie, the House of Representatives would vote in order to break it. If none of the candidates received a majority of the votes (more than half of the total), the House would choose from among the five highest.

The electoral college is still in use, although it has changed from Adams' day. One problem with the original system appeared when political parties began to develop during Adams' time. Because votes were cast without making a distinction between President and Vice-President, it was possible to end up with the two top officials of the country being from opposing parties, as was the case with Adams and Jefferson. Also, tie-breaking proved troublesome. In the election of 1800, Thomas Jefferson and Aaron Burr each received 73 votes. The House of Representatives had to decide who would be President and who would be Vice-President. It took 36 votes in the House before Jefferson was named President.

The 12th Amendment to the Constitution, ratified in 1804, solved these problems by separating the votes for President and Vice-President. Other changes have been made to the system over the years. Today, electors are nominated by the political parties within the states. When individual voters cast their ballots for presidential candidates in the popular elections every four years, they are actually voting for electors sponsored by the candidates' parties. Once the popular vote has taken place in November, the electors meet in December to carry out the ceremony of casting their votes and officially electing the highest officials in the land.

Many people have objected to the electoral college system because it introduces an extra step between the voters and their elected leaders. Critics of the electoral college say that this step is unnecessary. They also point out that the results of the electoral votes do not always match the popular vote. This is because the electors are pledged as a matter of custom and honor to vote for the candidates who receive the popular vote in their states—but they are not bound by law to do so. Some important elections in American history have been decided by the electors instead of by the voters.

John Quincy Adams received fewer electoral votes in 1824 than Andrew Jackson, but the House of Representatives chose Adams. The election of Rutherford B. Hayes in 1876 was determined by a Congress and Supreme Court electoral commission. Abraham Lincoln, in 1860, Benjamin Harrison, in 1888, Woodrow Wilson, in 1912, Harry Truman, in 1948, and Richard Nixon, in 1968, also were made President by the electoral college although they did not receive majorities of the popular vote. In some cases, victors in the electoral college have had only tiny leads in the popular vote; one famous example is John F. Kennedy, in 1960.

We can only guess how the course of history might have been different if all the United States' Presidents had been elected by direct popular vote. Today, the electoral college is the subject of much debate, as it has been for the past 200 years. Should it be changed? Should it be abolished? How would a direct popular vote affect our two-party system? Only one thing is certain: unless and until the Constitution is amended, the electoral college will be a crucial part of every presidential election.

he took it for granted that he would receive most of the votes. So he was hurt and embarrassed when, of the 69 votes cast, he received only 34 — less than half. The other 35 votes were spread around among a handful of candidates. But because Adams' 34 votes were more than those of any other candidate, he was made Vice-President. He was shaken, however, by the fact that he had not even been elected by a majority vote.

Adams soon learned that the second vote had been "scattered" among the other candidates by the persuasions and manipulations of Alexander Hamilton, a politician whom Adams first disliked and later hated; he once had called Hamilton a "worm." Hamilton was to be a thorn in Adams' side for many years, but the episode of the scattered second vote in 1788 irritated Adams forever. He hated what he thought of as sneaky, behind-the-scenes politicking; in addition, his pride had been deeply wounded. He complained in public about the incident, calling it a "stain" on the new country's honor. "Is this justice?" he wrote indignantly to Abigail. "Is there common sense or decency in this business?"

Although Adams may have been angered by the outcome of the electoral votes, he nevertheless hurried to New York

Washington, in the center, takes the oath of office as the first President of the United States in 1789. Vice-President Adams, just behind Washington's left arm at the right of the picture, was soon nicknamed "His Rotundity" on the floor of Congress. (Library of Congress.)

City, the temporary capital of the United States, to take up his new duties. In fact, he was in such a hurry that he arrived there before George Washington and was presented to the Senate fully nine days before the President was inaugurated. Senator John Langdon of New Hampshire, who was the temporary president of the Senate, led Adams into the meeting-room and said:

> Sir, I have it in charge from the Senate to introduce you to the chair of this House, and also to congratulate you upon your appointment to the office of Vice-President of the United States of America.

Adams received the official oath of office on June 3, 1789. At that time, the oath stated simply, "I, John Adams, do solemnly swear that I will support the Constitution of the United States." As soon as he had been sworn in, Adams administered the same oath to the senators. Then he made his formal inaugural speech. He talked about the successful formation of the federal union and the bright hopes everyone had for the future of the United States. He ended with a few compliments for Washington and for "those who had contributed to achieve independence"—and although he didn't say so, Adams surely included himself in that group.

HIGH OFFICE, LOW PROFILE

Honored as he was to have been chosen for his country's second highest office, Adams soon began to feel frustrated. He felt that he had no truly important work to do for the government or the people. Part of the problem was that no one was quite sure just what a Vice-President was supposed to do.

The President's duties were clear enough, of course. He

was supposed to run the country. But the only duty specifically assigned by the Constitution to the Vice-President was presiding over the Senate. This job was largely ceremonial. It made the Vice-President into a figure of authority but with no real function.

It is possible that the first Vice-President could have taken a larger part in the actual running of the government. Some people, in fact, expected the Vice-President to be something like a prime minister, a figure actively involved in making government decisions and carrying them out. But Washington did not encourage Adams to participate in the real business of government, partly because Washington did not especially like Adams, and partly because Washington felt that the executive power belonged solely to the office of President.

Also, Adams believed all his life that principles, not personalities, should determine men's success in politics. He disliked and distrusted those who schemed for power or who seemed too eager to seize it. Because he did not want to look like such a man, he often avoided opportunities to make himself more important. That is not to say that he didn't want to do more for his country—he did want to, very desperately. But he also wanted to be *asked* to. In the same way, he had a strong sense of pride and believed he deserved recognition for his labors, but he hated to look as though he cared about fame, so he refused to push himself into the limelight.

As a result, Adams' years as Vice-President were rather tedious and unsatisfying. Although he gloried in debate and speech-making, his post as president of the Senate did not give him the opportunity to declare his own views or try to persuade others to share them. His only chance to exert any influence in the Senate was in casting tie-breaking votes— which he was called on to do 20 times in eight years.

Nor did the President ask his advice on important matters. Instead, Washington relied on his Cabinet, which at that time consisted of five men: the secretaries of state, treasury, and war; the attorney general; and the postmaster general. Adams later wrote that he attended Cabinet meetings "only two or three times in eight years."

Blunders in Print

All in all, Adams found much with which to be discontented in his new position. He wrote to Abigail: "My country has in its wisdom contrived for me the most insignificant office that ever the invention of man contrived or the imagination conceived." This discontentment led him into several errors in judgment that blighted his first four years as Vice-President and made his later political career more difficult.

The first of Adams' blunders came to be called his "titles campaign." Many people remembered that in the *Defence of the Constitutions* Adams had said that no nation could survive without some recognition of its wealthy, capable, and well-born citizens. This and other statements were taken to mean that Adams believed in titles, aristocrats, possibly even kings. And Americans in general felt that such things were contrary to the republican spirit of their nation. (There had been some talk about making Washington a king, but no one took it seriously.) So when the new Vice-President suggested that America needed aristocratic titles, he created an uproar.

Adams was not the only one to feel that the new republic needed an element of stately showiness. In fact, one of the first debates in the Senate was over the way in which Washington should be addressed. One group suggested "Your Most Highness" (Adams agreed with this group), but straightforward "Mr. President" won out—and that is how the President of the United States is always addressed.

Adams, however, predicted that unless given the title "Your Majesty," Washington would be made fun of by European heads of state. He also said that the United States government should grant hereditary titles, like those of England, to people who performed great deeds for it; he claimed that this would be a good way of attracting competent men to public service.

Unfortunately for Adams, his observations about titles were completely contrary to the spirit of the times. Although he may have taken up the titles question simply because he didn't have enough real work to do, the results were troublesome. A few people questioned the strength of his republican (anti-aristocratic) principles. Most people, however, simply made fun of him, something he always took poorly. The newspapers ridiculed him in doggerel verse. Hamilton and others suggested that Adams really wanted a title for himself, and they gave him absurd nicknames, such as the "Duke of Braintree." Hamilton even poked fun at Adams' fatness by calling him "His Rotundity" on the floor of the Senate.

Adams bitterly regretted the titles controversy. He complained to the end of his days that his statements had been taken out of context and made to look absurd, and that is partly true. Adams' timing was poor, but his talk about titles reflected a genuine belief that people of merit must have some distinction. For his own part, he stopped wearing his ceremonial sword and powdered wig to the Senate and hoped that the whole tiresome business of titles would soon be forgotten.

In 1790 and 1791, however, Adams made matters worse with another error in judgment and timing. He read the writings of an Italian historian named Enrico Caferino Davila on the subject of the French civil wars of the 1500s. Adams was always impatient to air his own views on politics and government, and he now decided to write a series of essays based on Davila's history. Together, these essays are called *Discourses on Davila;* they were published in the Philadelphia *Gazette of the United States*. Adams said his goal in the essays was to examine the nature of the French state, but his true subject was human nature and its place in all states and governments.

Only a year or so before, in 1789, the French Revolution had overthrown the monarchy and set up a new republican government in France. Most Americans were overjoyed. They felt that the French people's choice of a republican government supported their own choice of a few years earlier, especially since many of the leaders of the French Revolution claimed to be inspired by the American Revolution. The French republicans, in short, were regarded as revolutionary brothers by the Americans.

In the *Davila* essays, Adams tried to dampen American enthusiasm for the recent bloody events in France. He pointed out a major difference between the American Revolution and the French Revolution: America had been a distant colony that had broken away from the parent state, while in France the existing order of things had been torn violently apart. He also predicted that the French people needed aristocratic distinctions in order to keep their society stable, and that the revolution would not stay alive. Finally, Adams suggested that the same was true of America. According to Adams, the desire for distinction and fame were universal features of human nature. He claimed it was impossible to erase all social distinctions, and the best that a republic could do was try to make sure that rank and distinction were awarded to people who really deserved them.

These views were not warmly received. They outraged the American supporters of the French Revolution, of whom there were many. They angered patriots who believed that America had a special place in the world and could never fall victim to the same historical processes that had destroyed other nations. They offended people who believed, as Adams did not, that human nature could change and improve under enlightened government. Finally, they raised the old doubts about just how good a republican Adams himself really was.

It would be hard to imagine a more imprudent act than writing and publishing the *Davila* essays in 1790 and 1791. Adams had never been noted, however, for keeping his opinions to himself for the sake of prudence. He believed that only by airing all thoughts on a subject could people arrive at the truth, and he often lived up to this belief in ways that made him unpopular.

But even Adams was finally forced to admit that he had gone too far this time. In the 32nd essay, he had said that people throughout history "had almost unanimously been convinced that hereditary succession [kingship] was attended with fewer evils than frequent elections." This statement caused such a furor that he ended the series of essays. Later, when he collected them into a book, he left the last one out.

Quarrel with Jefferson

The *Davila* essays were the indirect cause of a falling-out between Adams and Thomas Jefferson. Adams and Jefferson had been friends during the American Revolution and the Continental Congresses. Then, in the early 1780s in Europe, Adams had cooled toward Jefferson because the Virginian seemed to side with Franklin during the treaty negotiations with England. Now, after the *Davila* essays appeared, Jefferson wrote an introduction to a new edition of Tom Paine's book *The Rights of Man*.

In his introduction, Jefferson recommended the book as a good antidote to certain recent "heresies" (statements that disagree with popular belief). Although Jefferson did not mention Adams by name, everyone knew he meant the essays. Then, a series of letters, signed "Publicola," appeared in the newspapers, defending Adams and attacking Jefferson. Everyone thought Adams was writing the letters himself, but the author was really John Quincy, who was always loyal to his father.

Adams and Jefferson quarreled over the matter of the introduction and the letters. They remained enemies for many years — although the traditional image of America's Founding Fathers tends not to show their very human squabbles, disagreements, and bad habits.

After the *Davila* essays and the quarrel with Jefferson, Adams' political importance grew even smaller. Although he was re-elected Vice-President for Washington's second term (1793–1797), it was again by a narrow margin. He was probably elected partly because his name was still connected with the national events of the 1770s and partly because he was considered "safe": no one expected him to maneuver for power or to play much of a role in the government, and indeed he did not. His second term as Vice-President was, if anything, more boring than his first.

In the meantime, the nation's capital had been moved again, from New York City back to Philadelphia. Adams and Abigail had liked their comfortable house on Richmond Hill in New York. They were less pleased with their new residence on Bush Hill in Philadelphia. Abigail complained that it was hard to find a good cook in that city, and Adams fretted over the high cost of living.

During this part of his life, Adams followed a daily routine that changed very little from year to year. It included a big breakfast (with a long drink of hard cider), a daily walk, plenty of cigars, and reading all of the newspapers from front to back. To his sorrow, Abigail began to be ill from time to time. She frequently returned to Quincy, which both Adamses believed to be much healthier than Philadelphia. Adams missed her when she was away, wrote to her almost every day, and worried about his own health.

The years from 1793 to 1797 were a time of great disillusionment for Adams, because he felt himself more and more shut out from the important events of his time. The criticism he had received during his first four years in office, combined with the general uselessness of the post of Vice-President, turned him into something of a bitter, disappointed recluse. He spent less and less time with friends. Many remarks from these years show that he thought he had been badly treated by the government and the American people. Once, for example, he said that the people had treated the traitor Benedict Arnold better than the patriot John Adams. He also expressed fears about whether the republic would survive and prosper: "Mankind will not learn wisdom from experience," he gloomily predicted.

One bright spot in Adams' life during these years was his children. Although he worried about his daughter Nabby, whose husband lost a lot of money in a depression in 1797, he took pride in the careers of his three sons. (The fifth child, Susanna, had died when she was two.) Charles was a lawyer and Thomas Boylston was his father's secretary. But it was John Quincy, who had been appointed a diplomat to Holland in 1794, who was probably closest to his father's heart. He praised his son constantly and treated him with great respect, even addressing him formally as "Dear Sir" in his letters. He hoped that John Quincy would have a successful career in politics. "All my hopes are in him," Adams once wrote, "both for my family and for my country."

As his second term drew to a close, Adams grew impatient to give up the useless title of Vice-President. He took to writing letters to Abigail during Senate hours, and his thoughts turned to his farm. His letters were full of homey instructions: to wait until the roads froze before hauling the manure out of the barns, to gather seaweed for use as fertilizer, and so on. When the Senate adjourned in May of 1796, he hastened home to Quincy. A day or two later, he wrote in his diary that a gentle rain was falling to cleanse and refresh the tired gardens and pastures.

Chapter 7

The President

When Adams returned to Philadelphia in the fall of 1796, after a relaxing summer in Quincy, he had only one more session of the Senate to sit through as Vice-President. The next year would be the last of Washington's second term. And Adams thought it more than possible that he might succeed Washington as President, even though there was no law stopping Washington from running for a third term. Everyone suspected that "the Father of His Country" had had enough of being its President and wanted to retire to his home at Mount Vernon.

During his second term, Washington had been the target of attacks in the press by critics who disagreed with his actions. France and England were fighting, and Washington had insisted on remaining neutral. Some Americans, including Hamilton, favored the idea of war against England on the side of France. This opposition did not encourage Washington to run for a third term. As soon as the government had gathered in September, he announced, in his "Farewell Address," that he would retire in 1797.

Of course, everyone had already been busy with speculation about who would take Washington's place as President. Many people assumed that Adams, as the Vice-President, was the logical choice to follow in Washington's footsteps, a view that Adams shared. Jefferson was another strong candidate, but Jefferson made no secret of the fact that he would yield to Adams if the votes were tied. Even though he and Adams were still on bad terms, Jefferson respected Adams' many years of service and felt that he deserved the presidency.

THE RISE OF PARTY POLITICS

Neither candidate campaigned for votes. Both were content to let their records of service speak for themselves. But although neither Jefferson nor Adams believed in "politicking," a new element had entered politics to make their campaign an ugly one.

When the Constitution was framed, it included no mention of political parties. The first two presidential elections had been contests between individuals, not between parties. In fact, many people in the 18th century disliked and feared the idea of political parties. There had been parties during the Revolutionary Era, of course, because some people had favored the Revolution and some people had been Loyalists. But now that the United States was an independent republic, it was felt that all of its people and politicians would naturally share the same ideals and goals. "Party politics" was held to be a dangerous thing that could easily tear a nation apart.

Nevertheless, within a few years there were two political parties in the United States. The issue that caused their formation concerned the very nature of the federal union, something that had been left a little unclear in the Constitution. Was the United States to be governed by a strong central government, whose powers could override those of the states, or was it to be a loose coalition of states, each with its own fairly independent government?

Those who favored the strong central government were called Federalists. Washington had followed a Federalist program, and Adams shared the Federalist beliefs. Hamilton was also a Federalist. The enemies of Federalism were called Republicans (sometimes Democratic-Republicans). Jefferson and Aaron Burr were Republicans.

As a result of the growing conflict between the two parties, the election of 1796 took on an abusive quality. Adams and Jefferson behaved like gentlemen, but the supporters of their opposing parties were not so well-behaved. They raked up every possible item that could be used against the candidates and published many scurrilous newspaper articles.

Even within the Federalist party, there were divisions. Hamilton did not want Adams to become President, because he was certain that Adams would not take France's side in that country's conflict with England. On the other hand, he did not want the Republicans to win. So he promoted another Federalist candidate, Thomas Pinckney of South Carolina, secretly urging the electors to vote for Pinckney. The states now had a total of 276 electoral votes to cast, and not one of the candidates appeared to have a clear lead. The election of 1796 promised to be an interesting one.

And so it was. When the votes were counted, Adams had received 71, Jefferson 68, and Pinckney 59. The rest of the votes were shared in small numbers by 10 other candidates. (Washington received two of the votes, even though he insisted he wasn't running!) Because Adams had received the largest number of votes, he was made President. Once again, however, he was humiliated by the fact that he had just scraped by in the election. Instead of winning by a clear majority, which would have shown the voters' faith in him, he had won by a mere three votes. He was furious with Hamilton for once more making it look as though he had been elected "by accident."

Jefferson, who received the second largest number of votes, was the new Vice-President. To everyone's dismay, a situation had come about that the country's founders had not

The New White House

The decision to move the nation's capital from Philadelphia to the District of Columbia had been made by President Washington during his first term. Later, of course, the capital city was named Washington in his honor. He asked Pierre Charles L'Enfant, a French engineer, to lay out a plan for the city. L'Enfant selected a ridge of ground on Constitution Avenue as the site for the ''President's Palace.''

A public contest was held for the design of the building. Although Thomas Jefferson and other distinguished Americans entered the contest, it was won by James Hoban of Philadelphia, who received a prize of $500. Although people later said that his plan was merely a copy of the Duke of Leinster's house in Ireland, that was untrue. It was an original design for a three-storied building, containing more than 100 rooms.

Work was begun on the building in 1792. Pale-gray limestone from Virginia was chosen for the construction. Because the whitish-gray building contrasted with the other red-brick buildings of Washington, it came to be called the White House by about 1809. When a fire set by the British blackened the walls in 1814, the White House's whiteness was restored with paint. Not until Theodore Roosevelt's time, however, was the name used on official White House stationery.

Construction work was completed in 1800, and President and Mrs. John Adams were the first residents. Adams moved in first, and wrote apprehensively to Abigail that the building was far from finished. Wet plaster was everywhere. When Abigail arrived, however, she made the best of things with her usual good cheer. She even used the great unfinished East Room as a place to hang her laundry to dry—much more convenient than taking it outside.

anticipated: the President and the Vice-President belonged to rival political parties! For this reason, and also because of the personal coolness between them, Adams took as little notice of his Vice-President as Washington had taken of him.

Adams took office on March 4, 1797, in Federal Hall in Philadelphia. (He and Washington were the only Presidents ever to be sworn in in Philadelphia because the capital was moved to Washington, D.C., during Adams' presidency.) He was driven to the ceremony in a gold-painted coach drawn by six white horses. He later regretted this fancy touch, saying that it only served to revive the old titles controversy, which he wanted everyone to forget. "His Rotundity" was "Mr. President" now. And in his inaugural speech he called upon the people to end party politics and work together.

FRENCH AFFAIRS

Compared with many other periods of American history, Adams' presidency was a fairly uneventful time. We do not think of him in connection with any particularly grand gesture or national achievement. As President, though, Adams faced a series of problems and setbacks, most of which he handled quite well. His crowning achievement was keeping the United States out of war.

Troubles between England and France threatened to spread to the United States. The two European nations were fighting over their possessions in the Caribbean, and each tried to get the United States to take its side. France was angry because the United States had made a new treaty of trade and alliance with England in 1794. Now the French began to regard the Americans as possible enemies. Adams was not inclined to favor the French Directory (the government that had been set up by the revolutionaries), and his anti-French attitude made him unpopular with supporters of France in both the Federalist and Republican parties.

Soon, the French took action. French ships began stopping American ships at sea and sometimes accusing them of aiding the British. And an official of the Directory said that all American seamen who happened to work on British vessels were nothing more than "pirates." Before long, Adams decided to send a commission of three men to France. Their goal was to make a treaty in order to end this insulting behavior.

The commissioners Adams selected were Charles Cotesworth Pinckney, Elbridge Gerry, and John Marshall. They arrived in France and arranged a meeting with three agents (representatives) of the Directory. To the astonishment of the Americans, the three French agents said that they would have to pay an enormous bribe in order to be allowed to talk to Talleyrand, the leading French minister! Not all the details of the matter were ever made clear, but the amount demanded may have been as much as half a million dollars.

The XYZ Affair

Naturally, the Americans were insulted and outraged. And when their letters reporting this business reached the United

States in the spring of 1798, Adams was furious as well. The letters referred to the three Frenchmen as X, Y, and Z, so the incident came to be known as the XYZ Affair. Soon the newspapers, coffee-houses, and public meetings of America were buzzing with alphabetical indignation. The XYZ Affair angered many Americans against France, and Adams' anger was as great as any. He told Congress: "I will never send another minister to France without assurances that he will be received, respected, and honored as the representative of a great, free, powerful, and independent nation."

Despite his anger, Adams refused to take any hasty, rash actions. He wanted to proceed carefully and to be prepared for whatever might happen. He insisted on going ahead with preparations for war while trying to reopen negotiations for peace. Sadly, Adams found that thoughtful moderation does not appeal to the public imagination. The people who wanted to go to war with France were disappointed with him for wanting to make peace. The supporters of France (or enemies of England) were irritated that he wanted to be prepared for war. If it is true, as the saying goes, that you can't please everyone all the time, Adams was in the uncomfortable position of pleasing almost no one most of the time.

One result of the war scare was the creation of the American navy. As tensions grew in Europe, Adams was more and more convinced that a strong navy was necessary for the nation's security. He was pleased when the first United States naval vessel, the *United States,* was launched in Philadelphia in 1797. Later that year, the famous frigate *Constitution* ("Old Ironsides") was launched. By 1798, Adams had persuaded Congress to appoint a secretary of the navy (the secretary of war had formerly been responsible for both the army and the navy). Adams swore in Benjamin Stoddert as the first naval secretary in June of that year.

The attacks upon Adams for his anti-French stand

*Sculptor Daniel Chester French created this bust of Adams,
which stands in the Capitol Building in Washington, D.C.*
(Library of Congress.)

resulted in one of the most unpopular acts of his presidency, the signing into law in 1798 of the Alien and Sedition Acts. These acts made certain kinds of criticism of the government illegal. Writing or publishing statements against the government or in favor of France could be punished by fines or even imprisonment. The acts themselves were criticized by almost everyone, even though they were not strongly enforced. A few years later, under a new President, they were quietly repealed (cancelled).

Talleyrand, in the meantime, apologized to the United States, saying that X, Y, and Z were not really government agents but merely greedy impostors. He announced that he was more than ready to talk to any American commissioner. Eventually, negotiations were reopened, and Adams managed to keep the United States out of war with France. He had the wisdom to see that the costs of war, in both men and money, would be too great for the new nation to bear. He also believed that the United States should try every means possible to live in peace with other countries. He therefore signed a treaty of peace with Napoleon Bonaparte, the First Consul of France, in 1800.

ADAMS' ACHIEVEMENTS

The Adams administration included a number of other interesting or important events. Among them were:

- The creation of the Mississippi Territory on the western frontier in 1798.
- An epidemic of yellow fever in Philadelphia in 1798, during which the capital was temporarily moved to Trenton, New Jersey.
- The creation of the United States Marine Corps in 1798.
- The establishment of the United States Public Health Service in 1798, after a yellow fever epidemic.

- A treaty with the Cherokee Indians in 1798.
- The death of George Washington and a period of national mourning in 1799.
- The establishment of the Library of Congress in 1800.
- The movement of the capital to the District of Columbia in 1800.
- The appointment of John Marshall as chief justice of the Supreme Court in 1801. One of Adams' last acts as President was to appoint Marshall, who served as chief justice for 34 years and helped shape many American laws.

THE COLLAPSE OF FEDERALISM

Adams has been blamed for the break-up of the Federal party, which collapsed in confusion after his term of office. The charge is partly true. Adams entered his presidency with no real grasp of party politics. Although he agreed with Federalist principles, he preferred to think of himself, like Washington, as the leader of the entire American people.

One early mistake greatly weakened Adams' presidency and the whole Federal party. He did not realize how important his Cabinet was to be, perhaps because he had had so little to do with the Cabinet while he was Vice-President. Instead of filling all Cabinet posts with loyal supporters, as later Presidents were to do, Adams kept most of Washington's incompetent Cabinet members, even though some of them openly disliked him.

It was not until late in his presidency that Adams realized that several Cabinet members opposed his policies; some of them, under the influence of Hamilton, actually worked against him. He then dismissed two of them, but the damage had been done: the Cabinet had failed to provide strong, unified support for its President. As a result, Adams appeared weak and the Federal party was split between Adams' supporters and those who wanted a new, stronger leader.

This formal portrait of John Adams as President was done by Gilbert Stuart, the foremost portrait painter of his day. Stuart became famous for his 104 likenesses of Adams' predecessor, George Washington. (Library of Congress.)

By the time of the 1801 election, Adams did not expect to be re-elected. His dismissal of the two disloyal Cabinet members had brought about a rift within his party, and he was too uninterested in party politics to try to heal it. As always, he did not believe that he should have to try to humor others, or that he needed to justify his actions. He had done what was right, and that was the end of it. And because Adams had no flair for speeches or gestures aimed at winning over the common man, the public tended to view his presidency as a time of strife and dispute rather than of achievement. Unlike Washington before him, he did not command the affection and loyalty of the people.

Adams came in third in his attempt for a second term. Jefferson received the most votes, followed by Aaron Burr. With Jefferson as President and Burr as Vice-President, the Republicans happily took control of the government in March of 1801.

Although Washington had attended Adams' inauguration, Adams did not attend the inauguration of his political rival (of course, Washington had not run against Adams). The only other presidents who refused to attend the inauguration services of their successors were John Quincy Adams, Andrew Johnson, and Richard Nixon. Instead of being at Jefferson's inauguration in Washington, Adams was at home with Abigail in Quincy.

For many years, John Adams had kept returning home to Massachusetts to retire to his farm. But each time he thought he was going to be able to settle down for good, a new call was made for his services. He had always answered the call and he had always done his best to do his duty for his country. Now he was retiring one more time. This time his peace would not be interrupted.

Chapter 8

The "Old Man"

At 65 years of age, the "Old Man" (as he called himself) had come home for good. He planned to spend his retirement reading, writing, and farming – but he did not expect that retirement to last for a quarter of a century.

Both Adams and Abigail were glad to be settled again in their beloved Quincy home. The past few years had been difficult ones for the family. Abigail's illnesses had become more frequent. Adams, of course, had suffered from the strains of the vice-presidency and the presidency – he also suffered from the disappointment of not being re-elected. Saddest of all, Adams and his wife had serious worries about two of their children.

THE CHILDREN

Nabby and her husband, Colonel Smith, led a precarious and flighty life, often in debt and often moving from house to house. They had a shortage of money, but no shortage of children. ("There will be statesmen in plenty, if Mrs. Smith goes from year to year in this way," a relative had once joked.) Adams and Abigail often wondered whether Nabby and her children would have a comfortable, secure future.

The case of Charles Adams was more tragic. He had begun as a promising law student in the New York City office of Alexander Hamilton. (Although Adams hated Hamilton's

An American Dynasty: The Adams Family

John Adams was more than a patriot and a President. He was also a true patriarch, the head of a family that made important contributions to American politics and culture for many generations after his death.

The most noteworthy member of the second generation of the Adams dynasty was, of course, John Quincy Adams (1767–1848). Before becoming the sixth President of the United States, he served as secretary of state under President James Monroe and helped to acquire Florida. After his presidency, he held a seat in the House of Representatives, where he vigorously opposed slavery.

The leading figure of the third generation was also a diplomat. Charles Francis Adams (1807–1886) was John Quincy Adams' son. During the Civil War, he was the North's ambassador to London and played an important part in keeping England neutral during the conflict. He also edited his father's memoirs for publication.

Charles' four sons, the fourth generation from John Adams, were more active in literature and scholarship than in politics. John Quincy Adams II (1833–1894) served in the Massachusetts House of Representatives. Charles Francis Adams II (1835–1915) was a lawyer who wrote several volumes about the history of American railroads, as well as a biography of his father. Henry Adams (1838–1918) wrote a book called *The*

Charles Francis Adams, the son of John Quincy Adams and the grandson of John Adams, carried on the family tradition of diplomatic service. He helped keep England neutral during the War Between the States. (Library of Congress.)

Education of Henry Adams that compared the philosophies of Europe and America as they entered the 20th century. Published in 1907, it is considered a classic of American literature. Brooks Adams (1848–1927) wrote about Massachusetts history.

Others of John Adams' descendants to make their mark in public life included: Charles Francis Adams III (1866–1954), son of John Quincy Adams II, who was secretary of the navy; Charles Baker Adams (1814–1853), a scientist; William Cliflin (1818–1905), governor of Massachusetts; William Taylor Adams (1822–1897), who wrote children's stories under the pen name "Oliver Optic"; and Herbert Baxter Adams (1850–1901), a historian.

The tradition of public service and learning that started with the Puritan ancestors of John Adams carried into his descendants for many generations and helped shape American diplomacy and culture for more than a century.

politics, he recognized the man's skill as a lawyer, and perhaps he thought that sending his son to study with Hamilton would ease the strain of their relationship.) In 1795, Charles married Sally Smith, the younger sister of Nabby's husband. They had two children.

But while he had always been clever and charming, Charles seems to have been rather unstable. He reminded Abigail of her brother William, who had deserted his family,

John Quincy Adams, who became the sixth President of the United States after a diplomatic career, was a source of great pride and comfort to his father. (Library of Congress.)

stood trial for counterfeiting, and died an alcoholic. Like his Uncle William, Charles favored reckless, fast-living companions. He deserted his wife within two or three years (she and the children then lived with Adams and Abigail in Quincy), and he developed a severe case of alcoholism. Although Adams was later to say that Charles had been the greatest disappointment of his life, he made no attempt to see Charles in his time of deepest distress. He passed through New York City in 1800 without trying to see Charles, even though he knew Charles was desperately ill. Abigail did see Charles just before his death, possibly from alcohol poisoning, in 1800. She visited him in the dirty, run-down New York hotel where he later died. The sad circumstances of Charles' disintegration and death cast a shadow over the beginning of Adams' long-awaited retirement.

If Charles had been a disappointment, John Quincy was a continuing source of pride. After serving as a diplomat in Holland, he was transferred to Prussia (now Germany) by his father. When Adams failed to win re-election, he recalled John Quincy from Prussia to save him the embarrassment of being dismissed by Jefferson. But John Quincy planned to imitate his father by building a career in law and politics, and Adams believed he would be successful and would bring honor to the family name. This belief was correct—John Quincy Adams was the sixth President of the United States, and Adams lived to see him elected in 1825.

READING, FARMING, AND WRITING

The lifelong habit of reading was to be Adams' standby in retirement, especially in the first few months, when he needed time to rest and regain his peace of mind. He reread the classic Greek and Latin works he had studied at Harvard. Gradually, as the exhaustion of the past few years receded, he recovered his sense of humor. Having named his farm "Stony Field," he made fun of the once-painful titles controversy by calling himself the "Monarch of Stony Field," the "Count of Gull Island," the "Earl of Mount Arrarat," the "Marquis of Candlewood Hill," and the "Baron of Rocky Run."

During the early years of his retirement, Adams enjoyed physical labor and exercise. He still helped with farm chores, and he liked to ride his horse on the beach. He also walked four or five miles every day, often past the nearby Blue Hills. His one-time enemy, Governor Thomas Hutchinson of the Massachusetts Bay Colony, had lived there. Perhaps the daily reminder of Hutchinson turned Adams' thoughts toward the past. For whatever reason, in 1802 he took up his pen to begin a huge outpouring of writing. This time, he did not write about theories of government or constitutions. He wrote about his past.

Although Adams started an autobiography several times, he never finished it, and he touched on only a few periods in his life. Perhaps he simply missed the excitement of debate, for he abandoned the autobiography in favor of spirited exchanges of letters both to the newspapers and with private correspondents.

A HAPPY EXCHANGE

Adams remained critical of Jefferson throughout his two terms as President. Jefferson's foreign policy, Adams felt, was weak, and some of his actions harmed the New England shipping industry. Adams was also annoyed that Jefferson's government repealed some laws that his own government had passed, such as the Alien and Sedition Acts. Adams aired these criticisms of Jefferson in the newspapers and to his acquaintances, but he also reminisced about his friendship with Jefferson during the Revolutionary Era. Jefferson, too, made remarks that showed he still had some affection for Adams. Eventually, the two exchanged friendly letters in about 1811 and ended their long quarrel.

But Adams was unable to feel forgiving about Alexander Hamilton, perhaps because he had no background of long-ago comradeship with Hamilton to fall back on. His dislike of Hamiltonian politics took on a personal quality. All through his life, Adams had been unable to restrain himself when he had a pen in his hand. He had committed foolish and tactless things to paper with a fine disregard of the consequences, and he was no different now. He called Hamilton "a bastard brat of a Scotch pedlar" and accused him of "treachery" in turning his Cabinet against him. This violent dislike of Hamilton appeared in a series of letters that Adams wrote to the Boston *Patriot* between 1809 and 1812. These letters were an angry defense of his peacemaking efforts with France during his presidency.

In 1805, Adams had begun a long correspondence with Dr. Benjamin Rush of Philadelphia, another old comrade of Revolutionary days. They addressed each other as "Dear Friend of '74" and wrote about their experiences in the Continental Congress and afterward. Both men realized that the events of 30 years ago had already been forgotten, distorted, or turned into myth by many Americans. Adams once wrote to Rush, "I doubt that faithful [true] history ever was or ever can be written."

It was thanks to Rush that Adams mended his quarrel with Jefferson. Rush, who was friendly with both men, suggested that they write to one another to end their long estrangement. Adams' correspondence with Rush lasted until Rush's death in 1813. His death was a grievous blow to Adams, who wrote to Rush's widow: "There is not a man out of my own family remaining in the world in whom I had so much confidence, for whom I felt so tender and affection, and whose friendship was so essential to my happiness." Today, historians treasure the letters of the two men for the light they cast on the personalities and events surrounding the birth of the United States.

A Conflict of Opinions

Another of Adams' exchanges of letters was not as pleasant. In fact, it marked the falling-out of old friends. In 1807, Adams' long-time friend and neighbor, Mercy Otis Warren, published a three-volume book called *History of the Rise, Progress, and Termination of the American Revolution, Interspersed with Biographical, Political, and Moral Observations*. It was a lot of ground to cover, but Mercy Warren tackled it gamely. Adams, however, was far from pleased with the results. Not only did he feel that it contained some errors of fact, he was especially unhappy about some of the things Mrs. Warren said about him. Most upsetting of all was the accusation that when he came to office he had forgotten the republican principles of the American Revolution.

Adams replied in an angry letter that he had done no such thing. He pointed out that, initially, the Revolution had *not* been aimed at establishing an independent republic but merely at limiting Parliament's authority over the colonies. Americans had, as it were, been forced into independence.

From his own point of view, of course, this was correct. But Mrs. Warren was also correct in saying that some people, inspired by Tom Paine's writings, had hoped from very early in the conflict to create a new government in America. So the difference was less one of fact than of point of view. Nevertheless, the two exchanged a number of sharp letters, in which she accused him of conflicting with his own opinions, and he accused her of getting her facts wrong. The argument dragged on for months before Mrs. Warren ended it by saying that she would always think of Adams as someone for whom she had *once* had respect. Although they later made an attempt to patch up their friendship, they were never again on really good terms.

Another correspondent was John Taylor of Virginia, who wrote a book called *Inquiry into the Principles and Policy of Government.* Taylor's work attacked some of the points in the *Defence of the Constitutions,* which Adams had written during his ambassadorship to Britain in the 1780s. In a series of 33 letters to Taylor, Adams defended his old opinions, saying that there is a natural "aristocracy" or inequality in mankind that education can lessen but never erase completely. These letters to Taylor were to be Adams' last long work on philosophical or theoretical subjects.

THE LATER YEARS

Adams' life entered its final phase after 1818. His daughter Nabby had died in 1813, after an operation for cancer, and her husband died two years later. But the hardest blow of all was the death of Abigail, his devoted wife of 54 years, in 1818. Although Adams and Abigail had frequently been separated for long periods, theirs had been one of the happiest marriages of its time.

Adams remained vigorous in the later years of his life, although he lost his teeth and sometimes suffered from a palsy (trembling) of the hand, so that he was forced to dictate to one of his many grandsons or nieces instead of writing. He continued his reading, at first in the garden, with his dog Juno at his side, and later in his study. During these later years, he turned from serious and classical works to more light-hearted, entertaining books. He loved the historical romances of Sir Walter Scott, the stories of James Fenimore Cooper, and the poetry of Lord Byron.

But although Adams took up light reading, his interest in American government and politics continued strong. He read the newspapers, corresponded with politicians past and present, followed each change of party with comment and criticism, and continued to offer his views to anyone who asked for them—and to some people who didn't.

In 1821, Adams performed his last public service. He was invited to attend the Massachusetts Constitutional Convention in Boston. The purpose of the convention was to revise the old state constitution that he had written back in 1779. Although he spoke up vigorously to support or attack some of the measures that were discussed, Adams grew tired. Rather than arguing to his last breath, as he once would have done, he agreed to the changes that were made, and then he went home to Quincy.

During the final decade of his life, Adams took great pleasure in his correspondence with Jefferson. The two old friends, their differences now forgotten, exchanged ideas and memories in a fascinating series of letters that touched on everything from university education to the slave trade (Adams wanted it stamped out) to life after death (Adams believed in it; Jefferson wasn't so sure). The two men realized that they were among the last living relics of colonial times and the Revolution.

The Sage

Other Americans realized this as well. Many wrote to Adams to ask for his recollections of events long gone by. Others came to Quincy to visit, sometimes just to look at the "Old Man." At age 88, he wrote: "My old brain boils up, so many reminiscences of ancient facts, and conversations that I think ought to be committed to writing." But his writing days were almost over.

Adams' last service to his country was a toast that he

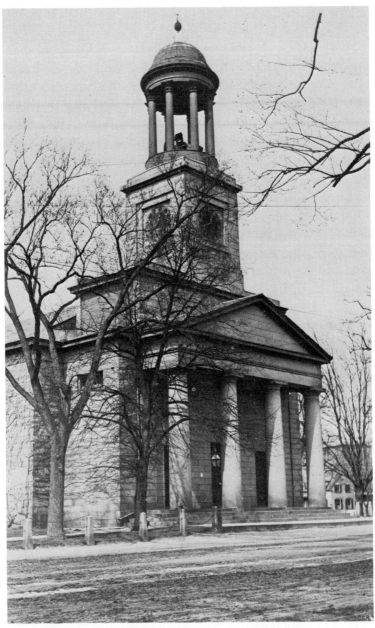

This photograph of the First Unitarian Church in Quincy was taken in 1908. Both John and Abigail Adams are buried here. (Library of Congress.)

was asked to provide at a local Fourth of July celebration in 1826. Over the years, he had come to resent the Fourth of July celebration. He thought it turned the complicated true story of the Declaration of Independence into a simplified public myth. He also resented the fact that all of the credit for the Declaration had gone to Jefferson; the stirring defense that had earned Adams the nickname "Atlas of Independence" had been all but forgotten. Now, however, he put his resentment behind him and sent the committee a toast to be used at the celebration. It was: "Independence forever!"

Adams died on that Fourth of July in 1826, the 50th anniversary of the signing of the Declaration of Independence. He was 90 years old. His last words were, "Thomas Jefferson still lives." He could not know, of course, that Jefferson had died in Virginia the very same day.

When news of the two men's deaths on the same day, the half-century anniversary of independence, was made public, an almost superstitious feeling swept across the country. One newspaper writer said, "Truly, there seems to be something more than accident in this coincidence."

Adams was buried next to his Abigail in the First Unitarian Church in Quincy. The Atlas of Independence had laid down his burden at last.

A PLACE IN HISTORY

John Adams is not remembered as a popular, much-loved President, like George Washington or Abe Lincoln. Nor was he a colorful, exciting character, like Teddy Roosevelt or John F. Kennedy. And Adams' time as President may seem less interesting to us today, because it did not contain some of the momentous events—such as the Louisiana Purchase or the War Between the States—that we think of as landmarks in American history. But Adams' contribution as President was a vital one nevertheless.

Tablets on the entrance to the Adams tombs commemorate the former President and First Lady. Adams' death, on the 50th anniversary of the Declaration of Independence and the same day Jefferson died, aroused a sense of superstitious awe throughout the land. (Library of Congress.)

When Adams became president, many people around the world (and many Americans, too) regarded the democratic form of government that had been set up in the United States as an experiment. The various colonies had joined together to fight for freedom from British control, but once the war was over, they faced the more difficult challenge of working together to make a stable country. George Washington had been able to lead the colonies and people of the new nation because he was admired as a war hero. Some even felt that Washington governed by the strength of his personality, not by the strength of the democratic system. It was up to the next President, John Adams, to prove that the new United States government could outlast its first leader.

Adams' time in office, though less eventful than some presidencies, added important stability to the young government. He demonstrated that the form of government established by the Constitution was an enduring system, not a short-lived experiment like the French Directory. And Adams' dealings with France proved that the American colonies had truly become a nation among nations, a voice to be listened to in international councils. John Adams, our second President, showed the world that the United States was here to stay.

Bibliography

Adams, Abigail Smith. *The Book of Abigail and John*. Edited by L. H. Butterfield, Marc Friedlander, and Mary Jo Kline. Cambridge, Massachusetts: Harvard University Press, 1975. This selection of the Adams family letters from the years 1762 to 1784 shows the warmth of Adams' affection for his wife and the interest she took in politics and public affairs.

Adams, John. *A Biography in His Own Words*. Edited by James Bishop Peabody. New York: Newsweek Publications, distributed by Harper and Row, 1973. Although Adams was never to complete his autobiography, this volume pieces together selections from his letters, journals, and other writings to give a vivid picture of his personality.

Allison, John Murray. *Adams and Jefferson: The Story of a Friendship*. Tulsa: University of Oklahoma Press, 1966. Illustrated with many old prints and pictures, this book gives a detailed account of the long relationship between Adams and Jefferson, who alternated between friendship and enmity.

Bowen, Catherine Drinker. *John Adams and the American Revolution*. Boston: Little, Brown, 1950. Many people consider this long and detailed book to be the best account of Adams' patriotic thoughts and deeds during the early part of his career in public service.

Butterfield, L. H., editor. *Diary and Autobiography of John Adams*. New York: Atheneum, 1961. For readers who want more of Adams' own words, this book presents his entire diary and his unfinished autobiography.

Chinard, Gilbert. *Honest John Adams*. Boston: Little, Brown, 1933. This biography focuses on Adams' political principles and on his sometimes difficult relationships with his fellow patriots. It was one of the first biographies about Adams to use material from his letters and diaries.

East, Robert A. *John Adams*. Boston: Twayne Publishers, 1979. This short, illustrated biography gives a good, basic overview of Adams' life and accomplishments.

Falkner, Leonard. *John Adams: Reluctant Patriot of the Revolution*. Englewood Cliffs, New Jersey: Prentice-Hall, 1969. Written for young adult readers, this account of John Adams' life gives special attention to the first half of his career in public service.

Kurtz, Stephen G. *The Presidency of John Adams: The Collapse of Federalism, 1795–1800*. Philadelphia: University of Pennsylvania Press, 1957. A detailed record of Adams' years in office, this book is also an account of the beginnings of party politics and party battles in America.

Shaw, Peter. *The Character of John Adams*. Chapel Hill, North Carolina: University of North Carolina Press, 1976. Shaw uses quotes from Adams, his family, and people who knew him to construct a portrait of the complex and often contradictory personality of our second President.

Shepherd, Jack. *The Adams Family: Four Generations of Greatness*. Boston: Little, Brown, 1975. This book is the saga of the Adams family's contributions to American politics and literature, beginning with John Adams.

Stone, Irving. *Those Who Love: A Biographical Novel of Abigail and John Adams.* Garden City, New York: Doubleday & Company, 1965. Though fiction, Stone's novel is based on years of painstaking research. Many historians regard it as a convincing account of John and Abigail Adams' life together until the end of his presidency. It is especially interesting because much of it is told from Abigail's point of view, with quotes from her lively letters.

Index